Getting Started in Bonds

Also available from John Wiley & Sons:

Getting Started in Futures by Todd Lofton
Getting Started in Options by Michael C. Thomsett

Getting Started in Bonds

MICHAEL C. THOMSETT

JOHN WILEY & SONS

New York • Chichester • Brisbane • Toronto • Singapore

Library of Congress Cataloging in Publication Data:

Thomsett, Michael C.
    Getting started in bonds / Michael C. Thomsett.
       p.   cm.
    Includes bibliographical references.
    ISBN 0-471-52480-8.—ISBN 0-471-52479-4 (pbk.)
    1. Bonds. I. Title.
  HG4651.T48 1991
  332.63′23—dc20   90-33830

Printed in the United States of America

10 9 8 7 6 5 4 3 2 1

Contents

Introduction: The Bond Alternative

"Stocks and bonds." The expression is so common that many people believe they are one and the same. In fact, though, the only thing they have in common is that they are both investments. Beyond that, there are many important differences.

Corporate expansion, city roads, schools, power plants, and even the national debt are all financed through bond issues. Companies and governments at all levels borrow money to investors, through bonds, to pay for their projects. So when you invest in a bond, you are lending money. The issuer has a contractual obligation to pay interest and to repay your principal.

In comparison, when you own stock, you hold a portion of the equity, or net worth, in a corporation. You are one of the owners. That entitles you to dividends and to any profit resulting from an increase in your stock's market value. You also take on the risk that the market value of your equity (stock) will fall.

This book introduces the bond market with a step-by-step approach. First, we explain what it means to invest in bonds;

next we examine and compare the potential risks and rewards. Then we explain how to figure the yield on a bond, and after that we describe the types of bonds you can buy. We wrap up with an explanation of information sources, alternative ways of investing, and how bonds fit into your portfolio.

Terminology in any specialized investment market is likely to confuse and frustrate anyone. The bond market is no exception. We deal with this problem in two ways. First, as a new word or phrase is introduced, it is in the margin. Second, all bond terms are summarized in the glossary at the back of the book. By seeing the combination of examples, illustrations, and definitions in the same place, you will be able to grasp the idea behind the phrase and place that idea in a context that has meaning to you as a potential bond investor.

This is a nontechnical book. Although you will need yield formulas to evaluate and compare bond investments, you will find the step-by-step approach, illustrations, and examples helpful in overcoming the complexities of this market.

A good beginning in the mastery of any investment is evaluating the potential rewards and risks. Later in the book, these selection criteria will be explained in detail. For now, you should be aware of the reasons that you might want to buy bonds. The rewards include:

1. *High liquidity.* One problem common to many worthwhile investments is that you can't get your money back when you need it, at least not without a delay or loss of some value. Bonds are highly liquid. They can be bought or sold easily, often with only a phone call to your broker.

2. *Fixed income.* Bond interest is fixed by contract, and payment dates for the entire holding period are known in advance. Thus, you can control and plan for your investment income from bonds far into the future.

3. *Return of capital.* The bond contract includes a promise to return your investment at a specific date in the future. In most forms of investment, final liquidation is up to you. The maximum term of the investment is finite.

4. *Minimum trading expense.*   A brokerage commission is charged for buying and for selling bonds, but it is relatively small. Compared to investing in real estate, annuities, or cash-value life insurance, bond investing is both efficient and affordable.

5. *Priority of payment.*   In the event a bond issuer is unable to meet all of its obligations, bondholders enjoy priority of payment over stockholders. Because the bond is a debt of the issuer, you will be paid first.

Bond investing also contains elements of risk, as all forms of investment do. There are four types:

1. *Default of the bond issuer.*   The issuer might be unable to meet its obligations, meaning you could receive only a portion of the amount invested or, in an exteme case, nothing at all. You can guard against this risk by investing only in bonds issued by the most secure issuers.

2. *Default or delay of interest payments.*   The bond issuer might not have the money to pay promised interest at the due date. The solution is to diversify a bond portfolio and to include a variety of other investments as well.

3. *Market risk.*   Between issue and maturity dates, bond values may fluctuate for a number of reasons. If you sell a discounted bond before maturity, you will have a loss. However, a bond may also carry a premium, in which case selling before maturity will produce a profit.

4. *Liquidity risk.*   If you tie up all of your money in bonds at what is considered a decent rate of return today, you might regret the decision later. If interest rates rise far beyond what you are earning, then your capital isn't free to take advantage of those conditions.

With the potential rewards and risks in mind, you can decide whether bonds belong in your portfolio. The decision to include bonds or to stay away from them should always be made on the basis of your personal financial goals and in consideration of your risk tolerance level. These important standards for all forms of investing are discussed in the last chapter.

This book is not intended to convince you to buy bonds, and it doesn't advocate bond investing for everyone. Our purpose is to explain how the bond market works. The premise is that you will be able to make a wise decision only if you arm yourself with information. We will show you how bonds work, explain the types of bonds and ways of buying and selling them, and compare risks among the different types.

We will provide you the facts every investor needs *before* committing money to any venture. With that information in hand, you will be able to decide whether your personal goals and desired risk levels can find a match in the bond market.

Getting Started in Bonds

1

Investing in Debt Securities

Communicating with someone who speaks a
different language is impossible, at least until
the two sides can agree on a preliminary vocabu-
lary. When you enter the bond market, you face
a similar problem. You need to master the
words, phrases, and concepts that will help you
communicate with others; to grasp the methods
for comparing and valuing bonds; to understand
the choices you face; and to evaluate risks and
opportunities.

In this chapter, you will find the groundwork
for understanding bond investments. We will
provide definitions of some basic terms, describe
the debt securities market, and suggest methods
for setting standards and deciding whether
bonds suit your own needs. Finally, we will suggest an approach to defining your personal goals,
selecting risk tolerance levels, and applying that
knowledge to bond investing.

DEBT INVESTING

debt security: an investment in which capital is loaned to a corporation, government, government agency, or other issuer.

Buying bonds and other debt securities is one of the three ways to put investment capital to work. The other two are buying equity positions and leveraging money. When you buy a *debt security*, you are lending capital to the issuer (a corporation or government, for example). You are entitled to receive interest payments and, upon maturity, a return of your capital.

issue date: the date a bond or other debt security is first placed on the market, which also identifies the time from which interest begins to be earned.

The contractual terms of debt securities and bank loans are similar. The company issuing a bond identifies a number of conditions and makes specific promises to bondholders:

maturity: the date a bond or other debt security becomes due; the date an issuer promises to repay investors' capital.

1. The amount of the loan (bond) is spelled out.

2. The interest rate is stated, and it will not change during the life of the bond.

3. Dates on which interest will be paid are scheduled from issue date through to maturity.

4. Maturity, the date on which capital will be returned to investors, is specified.

bond: a debt obligation issued by a corporation or other issuer promising to pay periodic interest and to return loaned capital upon maturity. Maturity occurs five or more years from the issue date.

A debt security has one important feature that distinguishes it from a bank loan: It can be bought and sold in the public marketplace or through auctions. Thus, a debt security has an element of liquidity and is readily marketable. When you buy a bond, you are the lender, but you can sell the contract to another investor.

Bonds and other debt securities can be compared by the length of time between the *issue date* and the *maturity date* (the date capital is returned. A *bond* is issued with a maturity of five years or more. A similar debt security with a shorter maturity duration is referred to as a *note*.

note: a debt obligation similar to a bond, but with a maturity date less than five years from date of issue.

Debt securities are not as widely understood

as is the second method of investing: purchasing *equity securities*—positions of ownership. The best-known form of equity security is ownership of shares of stock. When you buy 100 shares in a publicly listed corporation, you own part of the equity in that company. You also take an equity position when you invest money in your own business or buy a home.

In comparing bonds to stocks, be aware of the differences regarding your status as an investor, the time frame of the investment, and the type of income you will receive. These comparisons are summarized in Table 1–A.

Besides buying debt or equity investments, you can *leverage* your capital. This is the third way to invest. A small amount of money is deposited to gain control over a larger amount of money, and the whole amount is then put to work. Property purchased through leverage is usually pledged as collateral for the loan.

equity security: an investment in which a portion of ownership is exchanged for money invested, usually represented by shares of stock.

leverage: a method of investing in which capital is used to gain control over additional funds.

Example: You invest $20,000 as a down payment on the purchase of a $100,000 apartment building. The $80,000 mortgage loan represents the leveraged portion of your investment, and

TABLE 1–A Comparison of Debt and Equity Investments

Debt	Equity
Investors are creditors.	Investors are part owners.
The investment has a limited life.	The investment has a continuous life.
Investors receive fixed payments of interest.	Investors receive dividends declared each year.

the property is offered as collateral. Income from rentals is adequate to cover the monthly payment. The potential reward from leverage is a higher level of appreciation.

Each of the three ways you can use capital—debt, equity, and leverage—involves a different series of risks. In order to plan and control risk levels, you need to understand each series and determine whether or not it is acceptable to you. Looking only at the potential reward of any investment is only half the job.

Example: An investor is considering several equity, debt, and leveraged investments. His standard for selection is limited to the potential income—dividends from stocks, interest from bonds, and rent from real estate. However, by failing to also consider the *risks* of each investment, he is not making a complete comparison.

For an in-depth examination of the risks and rewards of bond investing, see Chapter 2. For now, the point is that debt securities, like all forms of investment, should be understood in terms of risk and reward—and in terms of the special features they hold.

yield: the percentage of return an investor receives, based on the amount invested or on the current market value of holdings.

face value (par value): the full amount the issuer promises to pay an investor upon maturity of a debt security; a market value of 100.

nominal yield (coupon yield): the stated interest rate paid on a bond, computed by dividing the amount of annual income by the bond's par value.

THE LIFE OF A BOND

The *yield* from a bond is the percentage of the face value, or the amount the bondholder will receive each year. So when a bond's *face value* (also called *par value*) is $1,000 and the contract promises to pay $80 per year, the bond has a *nominal yield*, or *coupon yield*, of 8 percent.

Bonds don't always yield the stated, or nominal, percentage, however. The face value will be *redeemed* at maturity date at 100 percent of face value (for example, a $1,000 bond will be redeemed for $1,000), but during the life of the bond, the market value may move above or below face value. The *current market value* of a bond may be at a *premium* (above the par value) or at a *discount* (below the par value).

Market demand causes bond values to change. The greater the demand for a particular bond, the more likely it is to sell at a premium. For example, a bond will mature in 15 years and yields 12 percent. Market interest rates are lower today than they were when the bond was issued, so that newer bonds yield only 9 or 10 percent. Because yield from the 12 percent bond is higher than today's average rate, demand for that bond will be higher, and its current market value will rise accordingly.

In comparing bonds, the nominal yield tells only part of the story. You also need to consider the number of years until maturity and the current market value: Is the bond selling at or near par, or at a premium or a discount?

The true annual yield from a bond is affected by the degree of premium or discount as well as by the nominal yield. During the period between the issue date and the maturity date, a bond may sell at a premium or at a discount, depending on market demand. And that demand will be affected directly by changes in interest rates as well as by other factors. Chapter 3, "Figuring the Yield," provides a detailed explanation of yield computations.

The life of a bond—including market value changes—is illustrated in Figure 1–1. In this example, the bond was issued in 1985 and will mature in 20 years. At the point of redemption, the bondholder will receive the par value regard-

redemption: the repayment of face value of a bond upon maturity.

current market value: the market value of a bond today, which may be at a premium (above face value) or at a discount (below face value).

premium: the current market value of a bond greater than 100; a bond currently valued above face value.

discount: the current market value of a bond less than 100; a bond currently valued below face value.

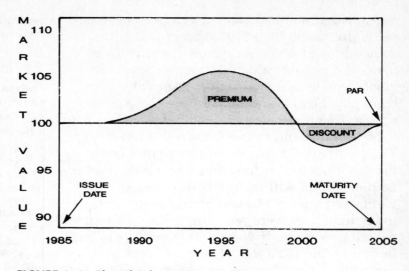

FIGURE 1-1 The Life of a 20-Year Bond

less of how much premium or discount occurs during the bond's life.

A bond's current market value is expressed as an index value compared with par. A bond currently selling at 100 is at par, but a bond described as being "at 96" is discounted to 96 percent of par. That means that a $1,000 bond "at 96" is worth $960 today. When a bond is described as being "at 104," the market value is at a premium above par, and the bond is worth $1,040.

Because bonds may currently sell at a premium or a discount, the nominal yield is less important than the *current yield*—the yield based on the current value of the bond.

current yield: the yield on a bond based on current market value; more accurate than nominal yield because it is based not on face value, but on value of the bond in today's market.

Example: Several different bonds pay nominal (stated) yields of 8 percent. However, the current yield will be higher when a bond is selling at a discount and lower when it is selling at a premium. Table 1–B, comparing three different bonds, illustrates this point.

Current yield is computed by dividing the amount of annual interest by the current market value. This yield will change each time the current market value of the bond moves up or down. Figure 1–2 shows the formula for calculating current yield.

At the point that you are comparing different bonds and evaluating their value as investments, the current yield helps make a valid comparison based on the amount of purchase and the actual rate of return. Remember, the *amount* of interest per year is fixed by contract and will not change. Current yield will change, though, because the current market value of the bond may be higher or lower than par.

The true yield on your investment depends on the rate of return earned (based on the amount you will invest and the interest you will receive). Of course, if your bond will be redeemed at par value and you pay more or less at the point of purchase, then your overall profit will also be affected. The time element must be taken into account, along with current yield and market value, to truly compare one bond with another.

TABLE 1–B Comparison of Three Bonds, at Discount, Premium, and Par

Current Market Value	Annual Interest	Current Yield
96 (discount)	$80	8.33%
105 (premium)	$80	7.62%
100 (par)	$80	8.00%

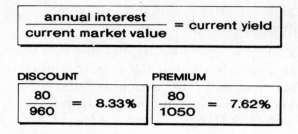

FIGURE 1–2 The Formula for Current Yield

CAPITALIZATION AND DEBT SECURITIES

The debt securities market is not as clearly understood as is the equity market. Most investors understand why corporations issue stock—to provide capital to pay for expansion, acquisition of assets, and investment in inventories. And thousands, even millions, of individual and institutional investors hold shares of equity in publicly listed corporations. But considering the equity value of a corporation or of a government, why do they also need to issue bonds? Why borrow money and pay interest to investors?

The answer is that equity capital, by itself, is not always adequate. Corporations and governments raise money for a wide range of purposes and for periods extending from one day up to half a century. Capital formation is achieved by transferring various forms of savings into utilization: money put to work by corporations to produce income, growth, or a combination of both; or money used to fund the activities of governments at many levels.

Example: The federal government funds the national debt through bonds, bills, notes, and other debt instruments. It also raises money needed for its immediate, short-term needs when tax revenues will be used to repay investors within a few months.

Example: A state government initiates bond issues to construct a waste treatment plant or a dam, to build and maintain roads, or to improve schools. Repayment is made from future tax revenues or specific fees.

Example: A corporation issues a series of bonds to fund a long-term expansion program. The money is used to buy millions of dollars worth of equipment, to build up the corporation's inventory of raw materials, and to pay for a growing level of annual overhead. Future profits are projected as more than adequate to repay the borrowed funds.

Governments and corporations repay their bond issues from different sources. Governments depend on tax revenues and, in some instances, income generated from operation or use. Corporations may determine that, since they will earn a future profit that is greater than the interest they will pay to bondholders, it makes sense to raise debt capital rather than seek more equity investment.

Capitalization can consist of both debt and equity. For example, a corporation may raise money by issuing bonds (*debt capital*) in addition to selling stock (*equity capital*). Some capitalization requirements are short-term, while others are longer-term.

Two examples of short-term needs:

1. The federal government issues debt securities to pay for current expenses; repayment will be made upon receipt of tax revenues within 90 days.

capitalization: the invested funds available to a company, representing all classes of capital stock, surplus, retained earnings (equity capital), and long-term debt (bonds).

debt capital: that portion of capital represented by debt obligations and excluding all forms of equity.

equity capital: that portion of capital represented by stockholders' equity and excluding all debt obligations.

2. A corporation needs capital to pledge a large purchase of raw materials. Funds will be available within 30 days.

money market:
descriptive of var-
ious forms of debt
obligations issued
by governments
and corporations
for which maturity
is short-term—one
year or less from
date of issue.

Short-term debt, defined as payable in one year or less, is broadly referred to as the *money market*. A wide range of federal and local government instruments, as well as corporate debt, falls into this category. The Federal Reserve and commercial banks dominate the money market and act either as issuers or as conduits for other issuers.

The range of money market instruments is summarized in Figure 1–3. Chapter 7 includes a more in-depth explanation of short-term debt securities.

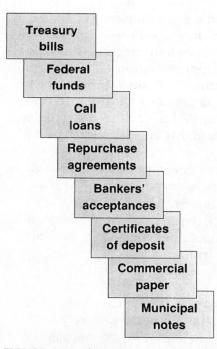

FIGURE 1–3 Short-Term Debt Instruments: The Money Market

Short-term capital requirements can be met through bank loans, notes, certificates, and working capital. Longer-term capitalization requirements are met through bonds, stocks, and mortgages, collectively referred to as the *capital market*. This group is summarized in Figure 1–4.

The combined range of all money and capital markets is called the *investment market*.

capital market: descriptive of bonds issued by governments and corporations with maturities of one year or more from issue date; also stocks and mortgages. Capital market instruments fund the intermediate and long-term growth of business.

investment market: the complete range of debt and equity instruments used to finance the capital requirements of government and business, including the money market and the capital market.

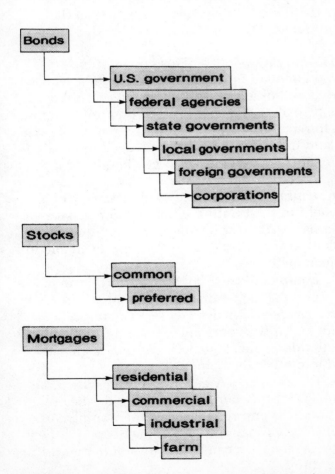

FIGURE 1–4 Long-Term Debt Instruments: The Capital Market

TYPES OF BONDS

Bonds can be divided into three groups: corporate, U.S. government (and government agency), and municipal debt securities.

Corporate Bonds

Corporate bonds are issued in four categories, with the distinction made on the basis of collateral—the assets pledged as security to the bondholder. The four types are:

1. *Mortgage bonds.* This common type of corporate bond is secured by a pledge of real estate. Bondholders' investments are protected by this pledge. In the event the corporation is unable to repay funds upon maturity, real estate will be sold to satisfy the debt or pledged to raise additional funds to be used to pay bondholders.

2. *Collateral trust bonds.* Bond issues are also secured by a portfolio of securities, which are held in trust until the bondholders have been paid. These securities can be liquidated or repledged if funds are not otherwise available to redeem bonds.

3. *Equipment trust bonds.* A third form of collateral is the corporation's capital assets. These assets are pledged as security for the bond, and if the company is unable to repay bondholders, the assets will be sold or pledged to obtain other financing.

4. *Debentures.* A debenture is an unsecured debt. The only security the bondholder has is the goodwill and reputation of the issuing corporation. Only those corporations with very strong financial standing can successfully offer and sell debentures.

U.S. Government Bonds

U.S. government securities are sold in a variety of ways. Some are sold at a discount, and interest is accrued throughout the holding period and then redeemed at face value. This is an alternative to selling at full face value and then paying interest every six months. U.S. government securities include:

1. *Series EE bonds.* These bonds are issued at a discount equal to one-half of face value and are redeemed at full face value several years later. They can be purchased in denominations as small as $25.

2. *Series HH bonds.* These bonds are issued at face value, and interest is paid every six months. The holding period is 10 years. They cannot be purchased for cash and are available only by exchanging Series EE bonds. Denominations begin at $500.

3. *Treasury bills.* A bill is actually not a bond but a money market instrument. Maturity is in one year or less—13, 26, or 52 weeks. Treasury bills are sold at a discount and redeemed at face value. Denominations start at $10,000, with additional multiples of $5,000.

4. *Treasury notes.* Notes are auctioned and mature in 2 to 10 years. They are available in denominations of $1,000, $5,000, $10,000, $100,000, and $1 million.

5. *Treasury bonds.* Bonds are auctioned. They mature in 10 or more years and are available in a number of denominations: $1,000, $5,000, $10,000, $100,000, and $1 million.

Prices and interest rates for bills, notes, and bonds are not known in advance, since they are sold in a competitive bid auction. In comparison, corporate bonds are sold at face value, and the nominal yield is stated at the time of issue.

U.S. government securities are among the safest of all investments, since they are guaranteed by the "full faith and credit" of the federal government. In addition to bonds issued by the Treasury, a number of U.S. government agencies issue bonds of their own. In most cases, agency bonds also come with the full faith and credit guarantee.

Municipal Debt Securities

The third major group is municipal debt securities. These include the bonds and notes of states, counties, cities, and towns, as well as issues by districts, agencies, and authorities. The three main classifications are:

1. *General obligation bonds.* These bonds are secured by the taxing power of a state, county, city, or town. Repayment to bondholders will be made through revenues from property, income, sales, and other taxes. General obligation bonds are secured by the full faith and credit of the municipality, and safety can be judged by comparing outstanding bond obligations to total future revenues.

2. *Revenue bonds.* This form of municipal bond is issued by districts, agencies, and authorities. Money is used to construct facilities that will generate future income. For example, construction of a transit terminal will produce future revenue from fares, and a toll bridge will be financed by a bond issue redeemed from future toll collections.

3. *Municipal notes.* These are short-term securities issued to finance operating expenses, most commonly when tax and other revenues collected within one year or less will be used to redeem the notes.

RISK TOLERANCE AND FINANCIAL GOALS

With the very wide range of bonds to choose from, and with the different degree of risks in the debt securities market, you need to ask yourself:

1. Are bonds an appropriate investment for me, based on my personal financial goals?

2. What portion of my total portfolio should be invested in debt securities?

3. How much risk am I willing to assume?

4. Should I buy bonds directly or through a diversified medium (such as a bond mutual fund)?

Your answers to these questions will depend on the types of bonds, their comparative risks, and the amount of investment capital you have available. No one strategy works for everyone. However, you can control your portfolio and establish your own approach by being aware of the three equally important sides of the investment strategy triangle (see Figure 1–5):

1. *Personal goals.* In the investment community, a "*goal*" is often described in terms of investment attributes: liquidity, diversification, preservation of capital, current income, etc. But in fact, these attributes define risks, not goals. A *goal* is more personal. Your immediate goals may include building an emergency reserve fund in a very liquid investment; saving money to

goal: a short-term or long-term result planned for by selection of investments and identification of acceptable risks.

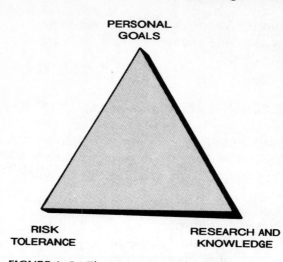

FIGURE 1–5 The Investment Strategy Triangle

purchase a home; renovating the home you already own; paying off a mortgage; paying for your child's education; starting your own business; or accumulating a portfolio for a secure retirement.

Goals dictate the desired outcome of an investment program and define the course you will take. Defining your risk tolerance level—through an examination of *investment objectives*—helps you to match specific investments with your goals.

Each individual goal dictates a particular type of investment strategy. If, for example, you want to save enough for a down payment on a home within five years, it makes no sense to tie up your money in an investment you can't cash out for at least ten years. And if you are trying to save money for a secure retirement, you won't be interested in speculating recklessly with those funds.

investment objective: the identification of attributes associated with an investment or investment strategy, designed to isolate and compare risks, define acceptable levels of risk, and match investments with personal goals.

2. *Risk tolerance.* The second side of the triangle concerns risk. How much risk, and what
type of risk, do you consider acceptable? You
cannot completely avoid risk when you invest,
but risk can be managed.

Risk comes in many forms, which are explained in detail in the next chapter. The most
common types are liquidity risk (the inability to
get your money out when you need it); diversification risk (failing to place portions of your portfolio in different areas); and inflation risk (the
risk that the buying power of your investment
will deteriorate over time).

All too often, investors make decisions based
only on yield or on the recommendation of an
adviser. The question of risk should always be
raised as well, because a decision will not be
suitable unless the risk level is acceptable to you
—within the boundaries of what is called your
"risk tolerance."

3. *Research and knowledge.* The third side
of the triangle is information. Once you define
your personal goals and an acceptable level of
risk, you then need to find investments that
meet your criteria.

You may depend on advice from stockbrokers
or financial advisers, as long as they match your
goals and risk standards to the investments they
recommend. But chances are that you will have
to perform your own research and gain your
own knowledge, rather than depend just on
what others suggest.

There are a number of sources for information.
Bonds, for example, are offered with a credit rating, which defines risk level to a large degree.
You can read books, magazines, and newsletters;
send away for brochures from industry associa-

tions and regulatory agencies; and attend seminars and classes. Knowledge also comes with experience—actually investing money and learning how to read stock tables, monthly or quarterly reports, prospectuses, and the financial news.

The more diligently you research and the more knowledge you accumulate, the better you will understand how each type of investment works. And with knowledge, you will also be better able to understand your own goals and risk tolerance.

SETTING RULES AND LIMITS

Keeping the investment strategy triangle in mind, you can see that picking the best investments for your portfolio is a highly individual undertaking. The discipline required for successful investing combines understanding and defining goals, risk tolerance, and knowledge.

This is true whether you decide to include bonds in your portfolio or to avoid them altogether. As a basic premise and approach to investing, definition, discipline, and consistency will help you to gain and keep a clear focus on where and why you invest. Collectively, these attributes make up the *financial planning* process.

financial planning: the process of managing investment funds and money-related matters for the purpose of achieving well-defined future goals; the plan is based on complete definition, discipline, and consistency.

You establish rules and limits by examining various forms of risk, such as liquidity, inflation and tax risk, and diversification. Some risks are minimized by the exceptionally high financial strength of a corporation, which for bonds is expressed in bond ratings. You can also reduce risk by investing only in insured or guaranteed forms. For example, placing savings in a federally insured account may be safe, but in exchange you receive a relatively low rate of interest. Likewise, U.S. government securities may be viewed as very safe because they are guaranteed by the full faith and credit of the United States, but if you tie up all of your money for many years in debt securities with fixed returns, you might miss future opportunities for higher yields.

In defining risk tolerance, remember the important differences between a personal goal and an investment objective. A goal represents the future outcome, such as purchasing a home, paying off a mortgage, or retiring with a secure income. An objective describes the investment and one or more types of risk. For example, an income mutual fund may be diversified, liquid, and professionally managed.

It is necessary to set rules and limits for yourself if you want to achieve your personal goals without violating your risk tolerance level.

Example: An investor was looking for a low-risk investment that would also beat inflation. She put her capital into an insured savings account yielding 6 percent per year, with interest paid and compounded regularly. This choice could have fit the definition of "low risk," but it didn't beat inflation on an after-tax basis:

The investor's combined federal and state tax rate was 39 percent (33 percent federal and 6 percent state). Inflation averaged 4 percent during the period money was left in the savings account, so, for every $100 in savings:

Gross yield, 6%	$6.00
Less: income taxes, 39% of $6.00	2.34
After-tax interest	$3.66
Less: inflation, 4% of $100	4.00
Loss after taxes and inflation	($0.34)

In this instance, the investor concentrated so much on having a "low-risk" investment that she actually lost spending power. A very important risk was not calculated as part of her plan. The solution would be to find a higher-yielding investment, one that would beat inflation and taxes. In exchange for the higher yield, it would be necessary to give up some of the other protection offered by the savings account, such as the fixed return and federal insurance.

There is a predictable relationship between risk and yield: The greater the yield, the more risk will be involved. Thus, a very unpredictable investment may yield much more than others do, but you also stand to lose a good deal of your capital. Also, some risks are hidden—an example is the loss of buying power, or value, of your capital. If inflation and taxes erode the real value of your money, then you are not getting ahead.

These concerns should affect the decision to buy bonds in several respects. First, you need to decide what your goals are. If you want to build a consistent base of income over many years, bond investing is one answer. If you want to speculate on future changes in interest rates or invest only with very secure corporations or governments, you can find appropriate bond investments.

Your goals and risk tolerance will also determine the method of buying bonds. For example, you can invest in savings bonds to create a regular income flow in the future, or you can buy shares of an income mutual fund or unit investment trust to combine tax benefits and a regular income stream.

TESTING RISK TOLERANCE

You can test bonds and other investments you
are considering for your portfolio in terms of
how they match your risk tolerance. When reviewing and comparing investments, ask these
questions:

1. *Is my portfolio adequately diversified?*
One danger every investor faces is failing to diversify. For example, if all of your money is invested in volatile stocks and the stock market
loses several hundred points, you will lose a
substantial part of your capital.

Diversification can be achieved in several
ways. The most common is by splitting available
funds among a number of different investments:
savings for liquidity and insurance, stocks for
long-term growth, and bonds for fixed income,
for example.

A second way to diversify is by industry. For
example, a stock market investor may distribute
a portfolio among high technology, food industry, utility, and real estate stocks. Economic
changes will not affect all of these groups in the
same way.

A third form of diversification, and the one
most appropriate for investors with a limited
amount of capital, is pooled investing. Mutual
funds are designed just for that purpose. A
professional management team invests money
paid in by thousands of investors and builds a
diversified portfolio with a common investment
objective, such as current income, long-term
growth, or a balance between income and
growth.

2. *Do I have an adequate liquid reserve?* Before placing money into long-term investments, it is wise to build an emergency reserve fund, preferably in an account that can be converted to cash without delay or loss of capital. This not only is a form of diversification; it also prevents unexpected losses.

Example: An investor places 100 percent of his savings in a one-year certificate of deposit. Eight months later, he loses his job and is forced to close the account. Under the agreed terms, he forfeits six months of interest.

3. *Have I examined and researched the risks?* It is fair to say that one of the most significant forms of risk is lack of awareness. Smart investors ask the right questions and compare unlike investments with the range of risks in mind.

Become an expert on the type of investments you make. The greater your level of knowledge, the better able you will be to make a valid comparison. For example, an investor who understands the risks associated with stocks, bonds, and real estate will be more likely to know what investments are appropriate, because all of the risks in each market are understood.

4. *Is this investment suitable for my goals?* Your personal goals should dictate the final decision for every investment. For example, the maturity of a bond can be timed for a deadline you have set for yourself for a future goal (college education, home purchase, retirement, etc.).

If your goal calls for long-term accumulation of capital, you cannot afford to speculate. So an investment that offers the potential for high return but that also comes with the risk of substantial loss will not be appropriate. Some advisers suggest, "Speculate when you're young.

If you lose, you will still have time to invest conservatively later on." But rather than investing on the basis of your age, it is more prudent to design an investment program based on both short-term and long-term goals.   **5.** *Can I afford a loss?*   This question will define risk tolerance very quickly. You may be attracted to a highly speculative investment, believing you can make a lot of money in a very short period of time. But remember: The higher-yielding investment is proportionately more risky. So you stand a chance of losing part or all of your investment when you chase fast profits.

Example: Boiler room operations sell varieties of options on commodity futures, which are very speculative. They like to quote fantastic returns: "If you had invested $5,000 one week ago, you would have earned more than 1,000 percent on your money." You will never get rich falling for one of these schemes. And you won't hear about a good deal during an unsolicited phone call.

6. *What am I really earning?*   Be aware of what your investment is earning on an after-tax basis. Only by constantly comparing yield *and* return between investments will you be able to select appropriate choices to meet your goals.

Bonds, in particular, do not always yield the nominal rate. Depending on the level of discount or premium, your actual current yield—and eventual capital gain or loss—could mean your realized return will be much lower or much higher than the nominal yield.

7. *Have I checked out the source?*   Whenever you receive advice, a recommendation, or an unsolicited sales call, always check the source *before* you invest. Millions of dollars are lost each year because investors fail to do their research or because they act not from a defined goal and understood risk tolerance level, but on someone else's advice.

When you ask the right questions, you allow your financial plan to rule. You know where you are going and what you will achieve when you arrive. You protect your capital. You manage risk and take control.

The next chapter explains risk and reward in the bond market. We will examine each type of risk and present ideas for evaluating many types of bonds in your own portfolio.

2

Risk and Reward in Bond Investing

Every investor wants to earn the highest possible yield and growth rate with the lowest possible risk. But maximum profit and low risk are not compatible attributes; they are in conflict.

As a bond investor, you need to be aware of the relationship between risk and potential reward, or opportunity. Risk in its many forms will determine whether an investment is appropriate for you, and it will also dictate the yield you will earn.

This chapter shows how to evaluate risk and make the decision to invest in bonds. We will also explain the many forms of risk that you face as a bond investor and how these risks can be minimized.

EVALUATING RISK

By identifying the risk associated with any form of investment, you also identify relative safety.

25

Your capital is at risk whenever it is invested; the degree of risk varies in a number of ways.

Evaluating investment safety requires a complete study of the two sides to risk. The obvious side of risk is the danger you face in taking a chance with your money. You may lose all or part of your risk capital; it might fall in value because of changes in demand, market factors, tax consequences, or inflation.

On the other side is opportunity. As the level of risk increases for an investment, so does the opportunity for higher yield. Risk and opportunity are directly and unavoidably connected to each other. If you want maximum safety, you will also have to settle for lower yields. Safety can be found in the form of guaranteed or insured accounts or the financial strength of the company. If you want to obtain maximum yield, you must also accept greater risks, represented by questionable financial strength of the company and the chance of default; volatility in price; or having your money tied up for a very long period.

The relationship between risk and opportunity is illustrated in Figure 2–1. When the scale is at zero, the investment contains the combined feature of low yield and low risk, but the opportunity side is minimal. And when the scale is higher, both sides grow. Yields are greater, but so is the potential for loss through one or more forms of risk.

selection risk: the risk that investment decisions will be based on the isolated basis of yield, name recognition, fundamentals, or general perceptions—to the exclusion of other valid measurements of risk.

SELECTION RISK

The first form of risk to be aware of is *selection risk*. This risk leads to chronic problems for

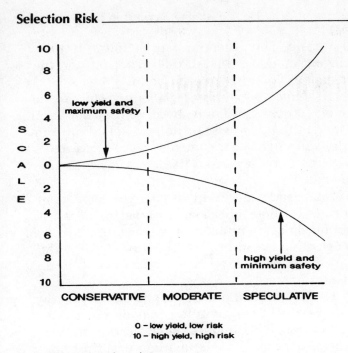

FIGURE 2–1   Risk and Opportunity

many investors, because the criteria for choosing one investment over another are misdirected. If you invest on the basis of well-defined goals and risk tolerance levels, and if you are willing to research the market, you will reduce the threat of selection risk.

Selection risk is best described by identifying the ways that many people invest. These include:

1. _Yield._   Investment decisions are often made only on the basis of yield, without regard for the risk level. When an investor uses yield as the sole basis for selection, the comparison isn't valid. For example, one bond yielding 6 percent might be more appropriate than another yielding

9 percent. The difference can be found in the current market value, the safety rating, and the degree of volatility of each bond.

2. *Name recognition.* Some investors decide to buy stocks and bonds because they are familiar with the company or its products. For example, you might hear someone say, "I invested in a Xerox bond because I like their copy machines."

Name recognition might give you some comfort, but it does not mean an investment is sound. For any number of reasons, the timing of a selection could be misguided or simply inappropriate for an investor's personal goals and risk tolerance.

3. *Recommendation.* Another popular way to invest is in response to someone else's recommendation. This includes a suggestion by a stockbroker or financial planner or a tip from a fellow investor. A recommendation might be a good starting point from which to perform your own decision tests and research, but you shouldn't be willing to commit capital without finding out more about the investment.

4. *Recent fundamental analysis.* Stock and bond market values change because of changes in reported earnings, dividends, interest rates, and other indicators, that is, the fundamentals. But by itself, analysis of fundamentals might not be the best way to judge the value of an investment. Other tests should be applied in coordination with fundamental indicators.

The current market value of a security will, as a rule, reflect the fundamental information that is already known. So when you review earnings reports of a company, remember that although the information indicates historical financial strength, it is not necessarily revealing about future market value, income, or growth.

5. *General perception.* You should never invest in bonds, stocks, mutual funds, or any other product that makes you uncomfortable. But in many cases, a perception of high risk is based not on solid information, but on a lack of research. Once you really understand the risks, you will be able to soundly select or eliminate an investment.

For example, some investors avoid the stock market for the wrong reasons. They may say, "My dad lost everything in the crash of 1929. Stocks are too risky." Or you might hear someone say, "I don't like bonds." What that often means is, "I don't *understand* bonds." The solution is to gain a more in-depth comprehension of the market, including an appreciation of the degree of risk in each form, and then draw an informed conclusion.

Perception can work against you in another way. If you have made a lot of money investing in a particular market, you might be unaware of some risks associated with it. Before the 600-point drop in stock market values in 1987, a number of investors put their capital into high-risk stocks and—for a while—earned significant paper profits. When values fell rapidly, the real risks became apparent, but it was too late for those who had not been aware of the risks.

MARKET RISK

One risk is common to every form of investment and is most apparent for products traded on public exchanges: *market risk*. Corporate bond

market risk: the risk that a bond's price will change on the basis of supply and demand factors, rating of the issuer's financial strength, and market interest rates.

market prices will vary on the basis of actual earnings levels as well as on the expectation of earnings levels. For example, if analysts predict that a corporation will earn $4.25 per share during the year and actual earnings come in at only $3.00, that will be perceived as a negative result —even if $3.00 per share represents a decent earnings level. In market risk, the anticipation of results may be more important than the results themselves, and it may have an even greater effect on changing price levels.

Earnings are watched closely by bond analysts and investors, because the company's ability to honor its commitment for interest payments and principal payments depends on cash flow and positive earnings. A company that is considered to be financially secure today could deteriorate in its competitive stance within a few years, affecting the market value of long-term bonds.

Three factors determine price and current market value of bonds:

1. *Supply and demand.* A bond that offers yields above the average current interest rate for comparable quality will be more in demand than one offering yields at or below prevailing rates. When demand is greater than the available supply, the market value will be driven up even further.

2. *Ratings.* When a company's bonds are rated as extremely safe, the market value responds. A low-rated bond may yield an attractive current rate, based on a comparison of discount and nominal yield, if only to attract investors; the higher rate is necessary to offset the lower demand for that bond.

3. *Prevailing interest rates.* As current interest rates increase or decrease, bond market val-

ues change. For example, if a long-term bond
yields a nominal rate of 7 percent but other interest rates climb to 9 or 10 percent, then the 7
percent bond is less attractive. Its market value
will fall, and the bond will be discounted. The
discount makes the bond attractive to investors.
But if you purchase a bond at par and its market
value falls, then your investment value falls as
well.

Market risk can also work out as a market opportunity. For example, the same 7 percent bond
will increase in market value if prevailing rates
slip below 7 percent. When that happens, a 7
percent yield is more attractive than the prevailing lower rates, so the market value of the bond
rises in response. The bond you purchased at
par may have a current market value at a premium, so if you sell, you will have a capital gain
in addition to the interest earned while you held
the bond.

You can judge market risk by studying demand for newly issued bonds. One test, the
acceptance ratio, or placement ratio, is a comparison between bond sales volume and the
volume of newly offered bonds. This is a measurement of current market sentiment rather than
a test of individual bond issues. The higher the
ratio, the more positive the indicator. If the ratio
is 90 percent or higher, there is a very high level
of acceptance for bonds in the marketplace. The
acceptance ratio is published regularly in the
Daily Bond Buyer.

**acceptance ra-
tio: a method for
judging the market
for bonds. The vol-
ume of bonds sold
during a period is
compared with the
level of bond issues
available. The
higher the ratio,
the higher the mar-
ket acceptance.**

DEFAULT RISK

Every bondholder is a lender, and even though
the issuer has a contractual obligation to pay in-

default risk: the risk that an issuer will delay or fail to make interest or principal payments as promised, or that the full amount will not be paid on the promised date.

senior lien: an obligation that must be satisfied before other, junior liens. Example: Bond obligations are senior to the rights of preferred and common stockholders.

priority: the right of certain parties to be paid before other creditors or owners in the event of liquidation and default.

cover: the degree to which a bond issuer is able to honor debt commitments through earnings and cash flow.

bond ratio: a comparison measuring outstanding bonds as a percentage of total capitalization; the ratio may exclude bonds with maturities of one year or less.

terest and principal, you should be aware of *default risk*. The issuer may default in several ways: Interest payments can be missed or delayed; the capital might not be available upon maturity to redeem bonds on time; or only part of the total might be repaid.

Bonds are generally considered to be safer than stocks because they are *senior liens* on the assets of the issuer. Bondholders have *priority* over other investors in the event of default. If a corporation is forced to liquidate assets, bondholders will be paid before preferred and common stockholders.

Default risk can be minimized by investing only in bonds that are rated as investment-grade securities. These are the higher rating grades that can be assigned to bond issues. (See Chapter 9 for more information about bond ratings). Debt securities issued by the U.S. government are widely accepted as the lowest-risk bonds of all because they are backed by the full faith and credit of the United States. A default is very unlikely, so default risk is practically nonexistent.

One of the important criteria that rating services use in assigning a grade to bonds is the issuer's ability to *cover* (repay) the bond, a test applied to corporate and municipal issues. This refers to a corporation's financial strength and ability to carry debt capitalization with earnings, or a municipality's ability to pay interest and principal based on taxing power. Coverage for corporate bond issues is measured in several ways, one of which is the *bond ratio*—the amount of debt capital the issuer is carrying compared to total capitalization.

In some applications of the bond ratio, bonds and other debts that mature in one year or less are excluded from the calculation.

Example: A corporation has outstanding bonds worth $62 million. Total capitalization, including debt and equity, is $249 million. The bond ratio is 24.9 percent, as shown in Figure 2–2.

Like all ratios, this calculation is not conclusive until it is studied in comparison. The analysis can be performed in two ways. First, one company's bond ratio can be studied over a period of time. If the ratio is rising, meaning debt represents a greater portion of capitalization today than in the past, that tells you:

- A greater amount of profits are consumed by interest payments.
- More working capital must be spent on debt service and interest payments today than in the past.

Second, comparisons can be made between different corporations. For example, if you are considering buying bonds issued by several corporations, a comparison of bond ratios today and in the past may indicate the relative financial strengths and weaknesses of each issuer.

The higher the percentage of outstanding bonds to total capitalization, the greater the default risk is in many cases. There are exceptions. A financially strong corporation can afford a

$$\frac{\text{outstanding bonds}}{\text{total capitalization}} = \text{ratio}$$

$$\frac{\$62 \text{ million}}{\$249 \text{ million}} = 24.9\%$$

FIGURE 2–2 Formula for Bond Ratio

higher level of debt capital and, in fact, may increase profits by increasing the bond ratio. If the company is able to produce profits that are higher than the interest cost of bond issues, then financing growth through debt capitalization makes good sense. The default risk arises when a company cannot afford to increase its debt levels, but incurs new debt just to repay old debt—a cycle that may eventually lead to substantial cash flow problems and reduced profits, and perhaps even to insolvency.

INFLATION RISK

inflation risk (purchasing power risk): the risk that yield from investments will not keep pace with the rate of inflation; the loss of real purchasing power based on changes in prices and yields.

The bond market, more often than most other markets, is closely identified with *inflation risk.* This is the risk that the yield from a bond investment will not keep pace with the rate of inflation, so that purchasing power declines rather than holding or improving.

The effects of inflation on purchasing power are often exaggerated. For example, salespeople like to use the Consumer Price Index as a measurement of an individual's inflation rate. But because that index is significantly affected by housing and transportation costs, you might not personally experience inflation at the CPI level. Unless you buy a new home and a new car every year, your actual rate is probably lower than what is reported in the CPI.

Inflation remains a substantial risk in the bond market, however, even if only as a "lost opportunity" risk. For example, you tie up your capital in a bond that pays a nominal yield of 7 percent. A few years later, it turns out that that

is a poor yield, as other bonds with similar ratings are paying 2 to 3 percent more. In this case,
you are earning less than you could earn in
other investments—thus, the lost opportunity. In
addition, your bond yield might not be keeping
pace with the rate of inflation.

This risk may be especially severe for long-
term bonds. You cannot know at the time of purchase whether the yield is high or low based on
changes in prevailing interest rates in the future.
The way to avoid inflation risk is to avoid committing a large portion of your capital to long-
term bonds or to adjust your holdings depending
on inflation trends.

Like many other forms of risk, inflation may
also be an opportunity. Say you tie in a yield on
a long-term bond today, and future rates are
much lower; then your investment increases in
market value. Changes in market interest rates
define demand and largely determine which
bonds have discounted or premium market
value. Short-term bonds are not affected by
changes in interest rates to the same degree that
long-term bonds are.

The danger in inflation risk is in not recogniz-
ing the loss of purchasing power. For example,
an investor buys bonds over a period of years on
the assumption that a fixed income at a given
level will be adequate to support a comfortable
retirement life-style. However, after many years
of inflation, it turns out that this assumption was
flawed. It will cost substantially more than the
investor believed to achieve a comfortable retirement from a fixed income portfolio.

The solution is to avoid extremely long-term
commitments of capital and to diversify the
terms of different investments. This gives you

flexibility as an investor and avoids the lost-opportunity risk that often plagues bond investors.

TAX RISK

tax risk: the risk that tax regulations or after-tax income will reduce the value of an investment, or that benefits available at the time an investment decision is made will change during the holding period.

Investors have become increasingly aware of *tax risk* in recent years for a number of reasons. Since 1980, Congress has passed a new, major tax bill once a year on average, and many of these bills have drastically changed the nature of investing and have affected everyone's ability to shelter income. Taxation and its effects have become a significant economic and valuation factor.

Tax shelters as they existed in 1980 have been virtually eliminated by changes in rules for deducting passive losses and by limitations on the amount of investment interest you can claim in any one year. At-risk rules (defining capital actually paid in to investment programs and recourse notes signed) have changed, so that it is no longer possible to leverage investment positions to gain maximum write-offs.

Bond investors face the risk that rules in effect today might be changed in the future. For example, Congress eliminated favorable treatment of capital gains as part of the Tax Reform Act of 1986. Other changes, including the tax-free nature of municipal bonds, alternative minimum tax, treatment of bond discount accrual or premium amortization, timing of the taxability of certain bond interest, and rules for tax deferral in IRAs and other retirement accounts could all affect the profitability of bond investing.

Other tax risks include audit risk, reporting complication, and the timing of reported capital

gains. Some forms of investment may mean a
higher profile and thus a greater chance of tax
audit. Calculating reportable interest and other
income from some investments may require
professional help. And depending on when you
close a position, the effects on your tax bracket
could be significant.

In evaluating and comparing investments, you
need to consider tax advantages and consequences in addition to yield, safety, and other
risk/reward factors. When tax risk is combined
with inflation risk, you will be able to identify
the _breakeven interest_ you will have to earn to
make a profit or move ahead—on an after-tax, after-inflation basis.

A primary purpose of investing money is to
keep pace with the rate of inflation on an after-
tax basis. Taxes reduce profits, while inflation
affects the buying power of principal. So the two
risks should be evaluated together.

**breakeven inter-
est: the amount of
interest an investor
must earn to break
even after income
taxes and after infla-
tion. To compute,
divide the assumed
inflation rate by the
after-tax rate.**

Example: You assume that future inflation will
average 4 percent per year. So your after-tax
yield from investments should be equal to or
greater than this rate. Your federal tax bracket
(the percentage you will pay on your taxable income) is 28 percent; you also pay 8 percent in
state income taxes. The total, 36 percent, is your
overall federal and state tax rate.

To calculate breakeven interest, divide the assumed inflation rate by your after-tax rate (100
less your combined federal and state tax rate).
The assumed rate of future inflation is 4 percent,
so breakeven interest is computed as:

$$\frac{4}{(100 - 36)} = 6.25\%$$

The breakeven interest formula is shown in Figure 2–3.

You must earn 6.25 percent on your investments just to break even after inflation and taxes. And, of course, in order to move ahead of the breakeven point, you will need to exceed this breakeven rate.

The calculation can be proven by testing it. For example, you deposit $100 in an investment paying 6.25 percent:

Amount invested		$100.00
Interest, one year	6.25	
Less: taxes (36%)	−2.25	
After-tax interest		$ 4.00
Less: inflation (4% of $100)		− 4.00
Breakeven		$ 0

Breakeven interest can be calculated for any tax rate and for any assumed rate of future inflation. The higher the tax and inflation rates, the greater the breakeven requirement will be. And that means that to achieve a breakeven, you will have to accept higher levels of risk (remembering that there is a direct correlation between risk and reward).

In extreme circumstances, you may have to decide whether to seek breakeven with higher

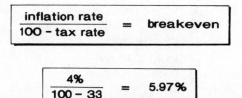

FIGURE 2–3 Formula for Breakeven Interest

levels of risk or just to settle for minimizing the reduction in your after-tax, after-inflation spending power. If risk levels are unacceptably high, loss reduction is a worthy backup position to assume.

Example: You are paying a high rate of federal and state taxes, and you estimate a high rate of inflation. But acceptable investments don't yield enough to earn the breakeven interest you have calculated. You select investments offering moderate risk and are losing 2 percent of your purchasing power each year. The alternatives are to lose more by taking no action at all or to choose other moderate-risk investments whose yields translate to an even higher reduction in real spending power.

Minimizing the loss of spending power may be the best choice available in some market conditions. Your only other choices are to take no action, which increases the rate of loss in spending power, or to take risks beyond what you consider an acceptable range and face the prospect of losing capital you can't afford to lose.

You can calculate breakeven interest by applying the formula to any assumed rate of interest and for any personal rate for taxable income. Table 2–A shows calculated breakeven interest requirements for tax rates between 28 and 38 percent and for inflation assumptions from 2 to 6 percent.

LIQUIDITY RISK

The ability to get your money out of an investment is called *liquidity risk*. A distinction

liquidity risk: the risk that it will not be possible to close an investment position without also accepting a loss.

TABLE 2–A   Breakeven Interest

Tax Rate	Inflation Rate				
	2%	3%	4%	5%	6%
28%	2.78%	4.17%	5.56%	6.94%	8.33%
29%	2.82	4.23	5.63	7.04	8.45
30%	2.86	4.29	5.71	7.14	8.57
31%	2.90	4.35	5.80	7.25	8.70
32%	2.94	4.41	5.88	7.35	8.82
33%	2.99	4.48	5.97	7.46	8.96
34%	3.03	4.55	6.06	7.58	9.09
35%	3.08	4.62	6.15	7.69	9.23
36%	3.13	4.69	6.25	7.81	9.38
37%	3.17	4.76	6.35	7.94	9.52
38%	3.23	4.84	6.45	8.06	9.68

marketability: descriptive of an investment for which an active secondary market exists, making it possible to find another buyer (the public stock and bond exchanges, for example); or an investment in which closing a position does not require finding another buyer (for open-end mutual funds or demand savings accounts, for example).

secondary market: the market on which bonds, stocks, and other investments are traded after the initial offer of securities; the public exchanges.

primary market: the market on which newly issued securities are traded, including government security auctions and underwriting purchases of blocks of new issues, which are then resold.

should be made between liquidity and *marketability*.

Bonds possess a high level of marketability in the sense that they are traded publicly and a secondary market for them is available. The *secondary market* is for bonds that have already been issued. In comparison, the *primary market* is for newly issued securities.

If you are willing to accept the current market value for your bond, you will have no problem selling it on the open market. But bonds do not always give you liquidity, that is, the ability to get your capital back. If you bought a bond at par and its current market value is discounted, you can sell only if you are willing to take a loss.

The alternative is to hold onto the bond until its value is at par or better. This could mean waiting until full maturity, which might be several years away. Be aware of the degrees of liquidity and marketability when comparing different investments:

1. Some investments lack both liquidity and marketability. For example, there may be no secondary market for shares of limited partnerships, and you might be unable to get your principal out before liquidation of the program.
2. Some investments, like publicly traded bonds, are highly marketable, but they could also be illiquid. You can close a position, but sometimes that involves taking a loss.
3. Other categories of investments may be both marketable and liquid. A savings account, for example, can be closed with no time delay. You receive your full principal (making it a liquid investment), and there is no problem with closing the account, since you don't have to find a buyer (making it highly marketable).

Measuring the activity of a bond is one way to judge market demand. Marketability may be relative. An *active bond* is traded in a way similar to stocks; the trading volume is high because demand is also high. In comparison, an *inactive bond* has a narrow, or thin, market. As a consequence of low demand, prices may vary widely or be depressed in comparison to active bonds with similar features.

DIVERSIFICATION RISK

Most investors understand the wisdom of spreading risk among several dissimilar investments. But *diversification risk* involves more

active bond: a bond that trades frequently, in high volume, and for which demand is high.

inactive bond: a bond that trades infrequently, in a thin, or narrow, market, for which demand is low.

diversification risk: the risk that capital will be placed in a narrow range of investment choices, so that an adverse market condition will affect the entire portfolio; or the risk that a portfolio's average yield will be low due to an overly broad mix of yields and risks.

than just the need to avoid putting all of your eggs in one basket. A diversified portfolio should be carefully managed and planned, so that you don't end up with a collection of losing, illiquid investments.

Example: An investor buys a number of stocks and bonds over several years. When stocks increase in market value, the investor takes profits, but when stocks remain at the same level or lose value, she leaves them in the portfolio. Those bonds that increase in market value are sold at a profit, but discount bonds are held for longer periods to avoid taking a loss.

In this case, a diversified portfolio ends up a grouping of losing investments. Profits are taken as they emerge, and capital is reinvested. By taking profits, the portfolio becomes very illiquid. Although investment buy decisions are diversified, the sell decisions are overly selective. The solution: Be willing to close positions that offer little potential for future profit as well as those that become profitable. Diversification risk includes the threat that your portfolio's potential for income and growth will deteriorate as a result of the way you decide to sell, perhaps to a greater extent than as a result of the way you decide to buy.

You may diversify your portfolio by type of investment (stocks, bonds, tangible assets, etc.) as well as by industry. And you may allocate part of your capital to conservative, moderate, and speculative investing. The broader your diversification strategies, the lower your overall risk will be. Another point to remember, however, is that broad diversification also equalizes overall profit and loss. Extremely high profits may be offset by extremely high losses in a well-diversified portfolio, so that the net result is a moderate return. With that in mind, you will be better off identifying an acceptable range of yields and risks and diversifying within that range, rather than offsetting speculative and conservative extremes with portions of your capital.

Even investors with a very small amount of capital can overcome diversification risks by participating in pooled investments. Bond mutual funds manage varying amounts of capital for thousands of investors and select a diversified portfolio of bonds; balanced funds combine bond and stock income and growth. Thus, for only a few hundred dollars, you can achieve tremendous diversification that is matched to your risk tolerance levels.

Even within a family of mutual funds, it is possible to diversify. Several investment companies offer a grouping of funds designed with specific goals in mind: aggressive and conservative growth, high current income, conservation of capital, tax-free income, and a balance between income and growth.

Transfers between funds in one family are possible with a letter or phone call. A transfer can be made to diversify or in response to changing market conditions. For example, you have about half of your portfolio in a stock fund, but you think the market is too high. Expecting a correction in the near future, you transfer away from the stock fund and divide your investment between an income fund and a balanced fund.

LEVERAGE RISK

When you borrow money to invest, you face *leverage risk*. While a higher amount of principal

leverage risk: the risk associated with borrowing funds to invest. This requires the generation of income adequate to continue repayments of principal and interest, accompanying the opportunity for higher income and growth from a higher level of investment.

offers potential for greater gains, you need to be
aware that the debt on that principal must be repaid. If your investment does not yield enough
to make repayments, then you face the danger of
cash flow problems.

Cash flow is the problem bond issuers face. By
borrowing money through a bond issue, they
must ensure that earnings will be high enough to
pay interest and, upon maturity, to redeem the
entire issue.

As an investor, be aware that leverage can be
a very high-risk approach. It may lead to the failure of an investment plan. Before tax reform,
many publicly sold limited partnerships de-
pended on leverage primarily to maximize tax
shelter benefits to investors. This was carried to
such an extreme that, in many instances, programs could not continue to make principal and
interest repayments. Income from properties was
insufficient for the partnership to stay in business.

To some people, leveraging is no different
from buying on the installment plan. Most people who buy homes are making a leveraged investment, and that's acceptable and widely
practiced. But when leverage risk is added to all
the other forms of risk you face as an investor,
you need to evaluate the decision from a different point of view. Ask yourself:

- What would a substantial loss in market
  value mean in a leveraged investment, compared to one that was not leveraged?
- Will *monthly* income be adequate to continue making debt repayments? (Most loans
  must be repaid in monthly installments,

while many investments do not yield income on the same basis. Most bonds, for example, pay interest only twice per year.)

- Will income exceed the cost of borrowing? If your after-tax interest expense is greater than your after-tax profit from a leveraged investment, the strategy makes no sense.
- Will the interest expense in the leveraged investment be deductible? With changes in tax laws, investors are limited in the amount of interest deductions they can claim each year. A leveraged investment that makes sense on a pre-tax basis might not look quite as healthy on an after-tax basis.

As an alternative to leveraged investing, consider depositing a consistent amount of capital each month and building your portfolio over time—within the boundaries of risk tolerance and based on your personal financial goals. This can be achieved in debt securities through mutual funds, for example, without having to involve leverage.

INTEREST RATE RISK

We have described *interest rate risk* in relation to other forms of risk. One variation of this risk is called *reinvestment risk*—the potential lost opportunity you experience when a fixed yield is low relative to future market interest rates.

Interest rate risk presents an opportunity in some cases; the yield you lock in by buying a bond today might be high by future standards. But if other market rates are higher than the

interest rate risk: the risk that prevailing rates will be higher than the rate earned from a fixed-income investment; or a decline in current market value due to changes in interest rates.

reinvestment risk: the risk that it might not be possible to invest interest and principal to earn yields comparable to a bond; that opportunities will be missed because capital is committed to a low-yielding fixed-income investment; or that investors will be unable to compound their returns from bonds.

yield on your bond, the market value of your bond will fall.

Reinvestment risk is an offshoot of changing interest rates. For example, you locked in your capital several years ago on a long-term bond yielding 7 percent. Today, market rates are about 9 percent. You could sell your bond at a discount and take the loss, or you could hold onto the bond, hoping the discount will disappear over time. In either case, you lose potential profits. Selling at a discount means losing part of your capital, and holding on to a low-yielding bond means missing opportunities in today's market.

Another variation of reinvestment risk comes up when a bond matures. If market conditions are lower at that point than in the past, you will be unable to find an investment with comparable safety features that yields as well as your bond.

Yet another version of reinvestment risk occurs when you receive periodic interest payments that you cannot reinvest at a comparable rate. You thus lose the compounding benefits associated with many types of investments, such as savings accounts and mutual funds in which you reinvest earnings by buying more shares.

You need to be aware of each form of risk and reward. You may face situations in which risk also poses a market opportunity, such as when future changes in interest rates could mean a significant loss or a significant gain.

The next chapter shows how risk evaluation can be expanded to the study of yields from bond investments. Nominal yield and current yield are only surface indicators for bond selection. You will also need to understand how to consider the time to maturity, the time value of money, and the degree of premium or discount to truly compare one bond to another and thus make an informed decision.

3

Figuring the Yield

Yield is the most obvious way to compare one bond to another. But if you ask, "What's the yield?" the answer often will be "That depends."

A bond's yield can be measured in several ways. It is possible that one bond will have a higher nominal yield than another, but the true yield to maturity will be lower; or perhaps a bond with a relatively low nominal yield will end up being a more profitable investment than one with a higher nominal yield.

Nominal yield, by itself, tells only how much interest will be paid each year. You also need to consider the time until maturity and the amount of discount or premium. These factors will determine the true yield on a bond to a greater extent than nominal or current yield.

This chapter explains how to figure the yield on a bond with the time and cost factors in mind. We will also show how to estimate yield using several shortcut methods and how to use bond yield tables. And we will explain total yield and net yield. The chapter ends with a discussion of the present value of a bond. This is useful for those bonds issued at deep discounts. Rather than paying interest twice per year, a bond accumulates value from purchase date to maturity.

NOMINAL AND CURRENT YIELD

In the last chapter, we explained how nominal and current yields are computed. Nominal yield is also called the coupon, or annual, rate. It's the rate the issuer promises to pay each year, based on face, or par, value. For example, a $1,000, 6 percent bond will yield $60.00 per year, with payments of $30 every six months. This is computed by multiplying the bond's par value by the nominal rate:

$$\$1,000 \times .06 = \$60.00$$

The nominal yield of 6 percent is expressed in decimal-equivalent form for this calculation. To translate a percentage to decimal form, move the decimal point two places to the left:

Percentage Form	Decimal Form
6.00	.06
5.50	.055
7.75	.0775

Current yield is computed by dividing the amount of annual interest by the cost or by the current value of a bond. For example, if a bond with a nominal rate of 6 percent is currently valued at 104 ($1,040), current yield is 5.77 percent:

$$\frac{\$60}{\$1,040} = .0577$$

The answer, .0577, is a decimal expression of the yield. To express this as a percentage, move the decimal point two places to the right:

Decimal Form	Percentage Form
.0577	5.77
.0600	6.00
.0775	7.75

The translation from one form to another applies to any calculation involving yield. To multiply by a percentage, you first need to express the percentage value as a decimal, and to translate the result of division, you need to express the decimal as a percentage.

YIELD TO MATURITY

Nominal and current yields give you a quick idea of a bond's current-year value, but these are not accurate measurements of a bond's real value over time. *Yield to maturity* (YTM) is what bond experts usually mean when they refer to "yield." This important calculation is necessary for several reasons:

1. *Discount and premium affect yield.* The discount or premiums have to be taken into account because they represent real adjustments to

yield to maturity (YTM): a calculation of yield that takes into consideration the discount or premium and the time until maturity.

your earnings. For example, if you pay $1,040
but receive $1,000 upon maturity, you will have
earned interest, but the premium represents a
loss of $40. And if you buy another bond for
$960 and redeem it at face value, you have a $40
profit above and beyond the interest earned during the holding period.

2. *YTM solves the problem you encounter in
trying to decide whether to figure yield on the
basis of cost or on redemption value.* If you
buy a bond at 96, you have invested $960; how-
ever, the bond matures at 100, meaning you will
receive $1,000. With that in mind, should you
calculate yield on the basis of the cost or on the
basis of redemption value? A good argument can
be made for either. Yield to maturity is based on
an average between cost and redemption values.

3. *Time affects your yearly average yield.*
The number of years until maturity will also affect the yield you actually earn. The shorter the
period until maturity, the greater the effect of a
premium or discount on the annual yield. And
the longer the period, the smaller the effect.
Therefore, the true yield of bonds with similar
discounts or premiums and the same nominal
rate will vary greatly if maturity is not the same.

Example: You purchase a bond with a nominal rate of 6 percent at a current price of 96,
spending $960. Although the redemption (matu-
rity) value is $1,000, you paid $40 less. Your
true yield will include a calculation of the annual average, including both $60 in interest per
year and part of the $40 profit.

Example: You purchase a bond with a nominal rate of 7 percent at a current price of 108,
spending $1,080. Redemption value is $1,000,
but you paid $1,080. Your true yield will in-

clude a calculation of the annual average, including $80 in interest per year, adjusted downward for part of the $70 premium you paid.

In both situations, the average annual yield will be affected by the number of years to maturity. The shorter the term, the more effect a discount or premium will have on yield to maturity. The true yield is the net of interest adjusted for discount or premium. The gain from discount is *accrued* or the loss from premium is *amortized*. Because your bond will be redeemed at face value, the amount of discount represents a *capital gain*, which is fully taxable. So if you buy a bond at 96, your capital gain will be $40. And the amount of premium represents a *capital loss* because you paid more than the redemption value. A bond purchased for 108 and redeemed at par will include a capital loss of $80. Interest earned during the holding period is *current income*. These distinctions are similar to profit and loss in the stock market. When you sell stock at a price greater than its purchase price, that is a capital gain. Dividends received while you own stock are current income.

Yield to maturity is a calculation of the average annual yield, including capital gain or loss *and* current income. Discount or premium is allocated evenly on the basis of the number of years to maturity, and annual interest is adjusted accordingly. Yield to maturity is actually the average of two separate yields:

Yield A: annual income, adjusted by discount or premium, compared with the purchase price of the bond.

Yield B: Annual income, adjusted by discount

accrual: the periodic recognition of profit from a bond discount, with equal portions added in each year in the term.

amortization: the periodic recognition of loss from a bond premium, with equal portions subtracted in each year in the term.

capital gain: profit realized when an investment or asset is sold at a price above its cost. When a bond is purchased at a discount and then redeemed at par, the difference is a capital gain.

capital loss: a loss realized when an investment or asset is sold at a price below its cost. When a bond is purchased at a premium and then redeemed at par, the difference is a capital loss.

current income: profits realized during the period an investment is held. Examples include bond interest and stock dividends. In comparison, a capital gain or loss represents the difference between purchase and sale price.

or premium, compared with the redemption (par) value of the bond.

USING BOND YIELD TABLES

You will not need to calculate yield to maturity every time you evaluate a bond. We have gone through the steps to calculating YTM manually for a number of reasons:

bond yield table: a table summarizing yield to maturity for bonds. One table is used for each nominal yield. The first column shows the price of the bond, and other columns show YTM for various maturities.

1. Knowing the method of calculation will improve your comprehension, making it easier to use a *bond yield table and* to understand what the yield reveals to you. Going through the detailed steps removes the mystery from the calculation.
2. A table might not be available at the time you want to calculate yield to maturity.
3. The table might not provide the exact maturity term or interest rate for the bonds you are comparing.

We previously calculated the yield to maturity on a 6 percent bond at 6.48 percent. This was the rate developed with the more exact method, averaging two separate yields. That yield was also based on a purchase at 96 ($960) with 12 years to maturity.

Figure 3–1 shows a bond yield table for a range of bonds yielding a 6 percent nominal rate. The first column shows the price in a range from 93.50 through 98.00. The next four columns show yield to maturity for 10, 11, 12, and 13 years to maturity date. Find the row showing the price of 96.00 and the column labeled 12 (years). The yield at that intersection is 6.48

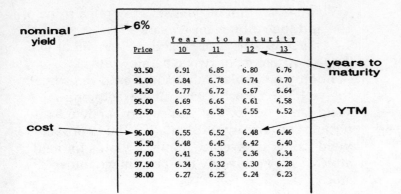

FIGURE 3–1   Bond Yield Table for a Range of 6% Bonds
(Discount)

percent—the same yield we calculated previously.

The same method is used for a premium bond. We calculated the yield for a 7 percent bond purchased at 108 with 6 years to maturity. Our calculation can be quickly checked by referring to a bond yield table for bonds yielding a nominal rate of 7 percent, such as the one shown in Figure 3–2.

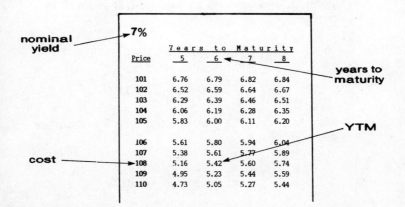

FIGURE 3–2   Bond Yield Table for a Range of 7% Bonds
(Premium)

The intersection of the row showing a price of 108 and the column for 6 years shows a yield of 5.43 percent—the same result we arrived at using the averaging of two separate yields.

Bond yield tables can also be used to estimate the yield to maturity when the exact nominal yield isn't shown. This procedure, known as *interpolation*, involves calculating the approximate yield using the average nominal yields immediately above and below the percentage under study.

interpolation: a method for estimating yield to maturity when nominal yield is fractional and not reported in bond yield tables. The YTMs for yields above and below the nominal rate are added together and averaged.

Example: You are considering purchasing a bond with a nominal yield of 6.25 percent. The price is 97, and there are 6 years to maturity. Your book of bond yield tables reports yields only in half-percentages, so you know the yield to maturity for bonds with nominal yields of 6.00 percent and 6.50 percent. But you do not have information on bonds yielding 6.25 percent.

The interpolation is as follows:

Step 1: Add the yields for 6.00 percent and 6.50 percent, at a price of 97 and with 6 years to maturity:

$$
\begin{array}{lr}
\text{YTM, } 6.00\% = & 6.61\% \\
\text{YTM, } 6.50\% = & \underline{7.12\%} \\
\text{Total} & 13.73\%
\end{array}
$$

Step 2: Divide the total in step 1 by 2 to find the average:

$$
\frac{6.61\% + 7.12\%}{2} = 6.87\%
$$

This is a reasonably accurate estimate of yield to maturity. Checking a book of bond yield tables, you will find that the yield for a bond with a nominal yield of 6.25 percent, currently priced at 97 and with 6 years to maturity, is 6.87 percent.

The same procedure can be used to interpolate the yield to maturity even for bonds with smaller fractional nominal yields.

Example: Your bond yield table book shows yields for bonds with nominal yields every half point. However, you want to estimate yield to maturity for a bond with a nominal yield of 6.125 percent.

In this case, the interpolation is:

Step 1: Calculate the yield for 6.25 percent, which is halfway between 6.00 and 6.50 percent:

YTM, 6.00% = 6.61%
YTM, 6.50% = 7.12%

$$\frac{\text{Total} \quad 13.73\%}{\text{Average} \quad 2} = 6.87\%$$

Step 2: Calculate the yield for 6.125 percent, which is halfway between 6.00 and 6.25 percent:

YTM, 6.00% = 6.61%
YTM, 6.25% = 6.87%

$$\frac{\text{Total} \quad 13.48\%}{\text{Average} \quad 2} = 6.74\%$$

The interpolated yield will not always match the actual yield precisely. However, for the purpose of comparing a number of bonds, this method will prove adequate.

Interpolation can be performed more precisely by figuring out the approximate interval between yields and then adjusting a known yield by the degree of change. This is known as the *professional method*. It will produce a more exact yield to maturity, but as long as you are only in-

professional method: a precise method for interpolating yield to maturity. Rather than averaging yields reported above and below the nominal yield, the interval between yields is calculated.

terested in making a consistent comparison between several bonds, the averaging method described above will be close enough.

Small variances should not concern you if you are only interested in evaluating yields between bonds. The important thing is to apply the same relatively dependable test to each of the bonds you are studying. However, be aware that the longer the term until maturity, the more variability you will find in calculated YTM—even using the more precise method of averaging two different yields.

Example: You are reviewing two bonds, one with a 5-year maturity and the other with a 25-year maturity. The calculated yield to maturity for the longer-term bond will vary from the percentage reported on a bond yield table to a greater degree than will the yield to maturity for the shorter-term bond. The value of capital gains and losses, if reinvested at the same interest rate being paid by the bond, will change over time. The longer the term, the greater the compounded rate of change.

The professional method is based on the assumption that yields can be reinvested at the same percentage as that yielded by the bond. Although this will not always be the case—market rates on other investments may be higher or lower than the fixed yield you receive—the assumption is a fair one because it is applied to all bonds under consideration. Thus, it can be used to make a valid comparison.

TOTAL YIELD

The importance of the discount, or premium, factor and of the time to maturity makes YTM an important calculation in the bond market. But there is yet another factor to consider in evaluating your bond investment: the effect of reinvesting interest received twice per year. We might assume that bond yield is isolated, that comparisons should be made strictly between bonds, but this ignores the fact that interest may be invested upon receipt, producing secondary income. *Total yield* is based on the assumption that interest will not just be spent, but will be put back to work in your portfolio.

total yield: the yield from a bond expanded to include an estimate of future income that includes compounding reinvested interest.

Compound interest will have a significant effect on the total return from any investment. When interest is reinvested, you earn interest on interest. The longer the period, the more rapidly interest grows.

If you are comparing bonds with identical maturity terms, the concept is academic. But chances are that you will review bonds with varying maturities. Thus, a similar or identical level of interest income will have greater value if interest is compounded for a longer period of time. You can apply total yield when reviewing bonds offering the same yield to maturity and nominal yield but different maturity dates. You can also test the validity of a bond investment depending on your assumptions concerning future interest rates.

Example: A bond will mature in five years and pays a nominal rate of 8 percent. The current price is 102. Yield to maturity in this case is 7.51 percent. You may assume that available interest rates during the next five years will be higher or lower than 7.51 percent. The actual outcome will represent total yield.

In order to test various outcomes, you need to know how to compute interest for partial years. Since bond interest is paid twice per year, let's

assume that your comparison will be made on a
semiannual basis. If you believe that you will
earn an average of 7 percent in the future, the
semiannual rate is 3.5 percent. This is calculated
by dividing the annual rate by the periods per
year (two in the case of semiannual compounding):

$$\frac{7.00\%}{2} = 3.50\%$$

If you assume that future interest will be 9 percent, divide the annual rate by the number of
periods per year:

$$\frac{9.00\%}{2} = 4.50\%$$

The same procedure is applied to calculation
of part-year interest for any compounding method.
The rate for quarterly compounding requires
dividing the annual rate by 4 (quarters) and, for
monthly compounding, dividing the annual rate
by 12 (months).

To calculate interest on interest for the next
five years, divide the 5 years into 10 semiannual
periods. At the assumed 7 percent, each $40 in-
terest payment will earn 3.5 percent per semiannual period (see Table 3–A).

Each period's interest on interest was computed by multiplying the previous balance by
the half-year rate of 3.5 percent (7 percent per
year divided by 2 semiannual periods). For example, the balance at the end of the third period
is 124.25:

$$124.25 \times .035 = 4.35$$

TABLE 3–A   Five-Year Calculation of Interest on Interest at Two Interest Payments per Year (7 percent)

Period	Bond Interest	7% per Year	Total
1	40.00	—	40.00
2	40.00	1.40	81.40
3	40.00	2.85	124.25
4	40.00	4.35	168.60
5	40.00	5.90	214.50
6	40.00	7.51	262.01
7	40.00	9.17	311.18
8	40.00	10.89	362.07
9	40.00	12.67	414.74
10	40.00	14.52	469.26

Interest earned through reinvestment is added to bond interest received in the next period. This total is then added to the previous balance to arrive at a new balance forward:

Interest on interest	4.35
Bond interest, next period	40.00
Previous balance	124.25
New balance forward	168.60

The outcome will be different if you assume you will earn 9 percent by reinvesting bond interest (see Table 3–B). In this case, the half-year rate is 4.5 percent (9 percent divided by two periods per year).

The difference between 7 percent and 9 percent over a five-year period is only about $22. However, when the same test is applied over a longer period, the rate of compounding accelerates, and the overall effect of reinvestment becomes more substantial.

TABLE 3–B Five-Year Calculation of Interest on Interest at Two Interest Payments per Year (9 percent)

Period	Bond Interest	9% per Year	Total
1	40.00	—	40.00
2	40.00	1.80	81.80
3	40.00	3.68	125.48
4	40.00	5.65	171.13
5	40.00	7.70	218.83
6	40.00	9.85	268.68
7	40.00	12.09	320.77
8	40.00	14.43	375.20
9	40.00	16.88	432.08
10	40.00	19.44	491.53

When you reinvest interest, your total return will depend not only on the future rate, but also on the time involved. Thus, as long as you apply the same assumption to every bond reviewed today, you will be able to compare bonds with varying years to maturity.

NET YIELD

An expansion of total yield brings another factor into the evaluation of bonds: income tax liabilities. This factor is especially useful when comparing taxable and tax-free bonds.

Example: You are comparing two different bonds. One is taxable and has a yield to maturity of 7.51 percent; the other is tax-free and yields 4.88 percent. Which is a better investment on the basis of the yield alone? The answer depends on your effective federal and state income rate.

Your effective tax rate is the rate you will pay based on your taxable income. The *net yield* can be computed on yield to maturity simply by multiplying that yield by the after-tax rate.

Example: Yield to maturity on your bond investment is 7.51 percent. Your effective tax rate is 33 percent, meaning your after-tax income is 67 percent (100 less 33). To compute net yield:

$$7.51\% \times 67\% = 5.03\%$$

Net yield can also be computed on the basis of average net income figured on the yearly averages used to arrive at yield to maturity.

Example: Your bond pays a nominal yield of 8 percent and was purchased at 102. It matures in five years. Your effective combined federal and state income tax rate is 33 percent.

Table 3–C shows the *average* annual income on an after-tax basis. But the $20 premium loss won't actually be recognized for tax purposes until the bond matures or is sold. It is more accurate to figure out after-tax income based on the year the loss is deducted (see Table 3–D).

net yield: the yield from a bond after deducting a portion of total income for federal and state income tax liabilities.

TABLE 3–C Average Annual Net Income

Year	Interest Earned	Partial Premium	Income	Less 33%	Net Income
1	80.00	− 4.00	76.00	25.08	50.92
2	80.00	− 4.00	76.00	25.08	50.92
3	80.00	− 4.00	76.00	25.08	50.92
4	80.00	− 4.00	76.00	25.08	50.92
5	80.00	− 4.00	76.00	25.08	50.92
Total	400.00	−20.00	380.00	125.40	254.60

TABLE 3–D Annual Net Income with Deferred Premium Loss

Year	Interest Earned	Less Premium	Income	Less 33%	Net Income
1	80.00	—	80.00	26.40	53.60
2	80.00	—	80.00	26.40	53.60
3	80.00	—	80.00	26.40	53.60
4	80.00	—	80.00	26.40	53.60
5	80.00	−20.00	60.00	19.80	40.20
Total	400.00	−20.00	380.00	125.40	254.60

The final step in this calculation is the combination of net, after-tax yield with interest income assumed to be reinvested every six months. Net income can then be broken down each year on the basis of assumptions about what you will be able to earn in the future.

Example: You purchase a bond for 102 that matures in five years. The nominal interest rate is 8 percent, and you assume you will be able to reinvest at the same rate. Your effective tax rate is 33 percent.

The detailed analysis in Table 3–E is most valuable when comparing taxable and nontaxable bonds. For example, yields on a corporate bond and a municipal bond might seem far apart, but when the corporate bond is analyzed for net yield, the two become more similar. Net yield will also affect long-term profits when the comparison is made between taxable and tax-deferred investing. For example, you may want to evaluate a bond's overall net yield in your personal portfolio and in an Individual Retirement Account, where profits are deferred until funds are withdrawn.

TABLE 3–E   Annual Net Income with Future Earnings Assumption

Period	Interest on Bond	Plus 8%	Less Premium	Total	Less 33%	Net Income
1	40.00	—	—	40.00	13.20	26.80
2	40.00	1.60	—	41.60	13.73	27.87
3	40.00	3.26	—	43.26	14.28	28.98
4	40.00	4.99	—	44.99	14.85	30.14
5	40.00	6.79	—	46.79	15.44	31.35
6	40.00	8.67	—	48.67	16.06	32.61
7	40.00	10.61	—	50.61	16.70	33.91
8	40.00	12.64	—	52.64	17.37	35.27
9	40.00	14.74	—	54.74	18.06	36.68
10	40.00	16.93	20.00	36.93	12.19	24.74
Total	400.00	80.23	20.00	460.23	151.88	308.35

PRESENT VALUE OF A BOND

Yield to maturity, total yield, and net yield are used to evaluate and compare bonds that are originally marketed at par and that may have a current market value at a discount or at a premium from redemption value. However, many bonds are not sold with a nominal yield based on par. Instead, they are sold at a deep discount. Interest is not paid every six months, but accrued throughout the term. At the point of maturity, the discounted purchase price gradually increases to redemption value.

This process is referred to as *accumulation*. You buy a bond with a face value of $1,000, but you pay only about $200. Each year, the current value of the bond grows, with the amount of growth based on the term and on the applicable interest rate. In most instances, you will know

accumulation: the gradual increase in the value of a discounted bond throughout the holding period.

present value: the
value today of a fu-
ture sum, assuming
a rate of interest,
compounding
method, and num-
ber of periods.

the face value and the interest rate. To calculate
the current value of that bond, it is necessary to
find the *present value*.

Example: A bond with a redemption value of
$1,000 is available in maturities of 10, 15, and
20 years. The yield is advertised as 10 percent.
What is the present value of each bond?

The answer is calculated by dividing the maturity value ($1,000) by the compounded rate for
the number of periods involved. Since interest is
accrued twice per year, the number of periods is:

10 years = 20 semiannual periods
15 years = 30 semiannual periods
20 years = 40 semiannual periods

The interest rate is 10 percent per year, but
because interest is accrued in two installments,
we must use a 5 percent rate for each period.

To figure the compound value of 5 percent for
a number of periods, we first add 1 to the decimal form of yield:

$$1 + .05 = 1.05$$

This is multiplied by itself for the number of periods in the term:

$$(1.05)(1.05)(1.05) \ldots (1.05)$$

When dealing with a large number of steps,
the calculation is expressed with a superscripted
number:

$$\text{10 years (20 periods): } (1.05)^{20}$$

The expression states, "multiply 1.05 by itself 20
times."

15 years (30 periods): $(1.05)^{30}$

The expression states, "multiply 1.05 by itself 30 times."

20 years (40 periods): $(1.05)^{40}$

The expression states, "multiply 1.05 by itself 40 times."

The formula for the present value of a bond is shown in Figure 3–3. Note that the maturity value is divided by the calculated compound value described above. Applied to our example, the formula reveals:

10 years:

$$PV = \frac{1,000}{(1.05)^{20}}$$
$$= \frac{1,000}{2.653298}$$
$$= \$376.89$$

15 years:

$$PV = \frac{1,000}{(1.05)^{30}}$$
$$= \frac{1,000}{4.321942}$$
$$= \$231.38$$

$$PV = \frac{M}{(1+r)^n}$$

M = maturity value
r = half–year rate
n = number of half–year periods
PV = present value

FIGURE 3–3 Formula: Present Value of a Bond

20 years:

$$PV = \frac{1,000}{(1.05)^{40}}$$
$$= \frac{1,000}{7.039989}$$
$$= \$142.05$$

You can prove that the formula works by going through the steps using most hand calculators. For example, to prove the 10-year computation, follow these steps:

Proving present value

Step 1: Enter *1.05*   (interest rate plus 1)
Step 2: Depress 'x'   (multiply)
Step 3: Enter *376.89*   (present value, beginning of the period)
Step 4: Depress '='   (present value, first period)
Step 5: Repeat step 4 for each period.   (present values of periods 2 to 20)

When this computation is complete, you will end up with a series of present values as of the end of each six-month period (there are 20 in the 10-year term), as shown in Table 3–F.

We can also say that the present value of a discounted bond yielding 10 percent per year is reflected in the number of years to maturity:

Maturity	Present Value
10 years	$376.89
15 years	$231.38
20 years	$142.05

Performing 40 calculations for the 20-year maturity is a tedious process if done by hand. How-

TABLE 3—F   Present Values in a 10-Year Term for a $1,000 Bond with an Advertised Yield of 10 Percent

Period	Present Value	Period	Present Value
Start	376.89	—	—
1	395.73	11	644.61
2	415.52	12	676.84
3	436.30	13	710.68
4	458.11	14	746.22
5	481.02	15	783.53
6	505.07	16	822.70
7	530.32	17	863.84
8	556.84	18	907.03
9	584.68	19	952.38
10	613.91	20	1000.00

ever, there is a way to quickly develop the factor you need. Refer to a book of compound interest tables and turn to the section showing factors for annual compounding at 5 percent. Using the table that shows the future worth of one dollar with interest, find the row for 40 years. You will find the factor for the 40 calculations required to compute the present value.

Note that the factor is listed as 40 *years*. Remember that we are figuring 5 percent return per *period*. In this application, we have two semiannual periods, each paying 5 percent. Using this factor is the same as calculating interest paid once per year at an annual rate of 5 percent. For our purposes, the "year" actually represents a semiannual "period."

The yield on bond investments can be interpreted in many ways depending on the assumptions you apply, the comparisons you make, and your effective tax rate. The important message to remember is this: Make your study on a consistent basis. Be aware of the effect of long-term interest on interest, and apply the same tests to each bond. If tax treatment is different for two bonds, be sure your evaluation takes that into account.

With the basics of yield, you are now ready to examine the various types of bonds on the market. The next four chapters explain the choices in corporate, U.S. government, and municipal bonds, as well as other forms of debt securities.

4

Corporate Debt Securities

Corporations raise capital through debt or through equity to fund expansion, to purchase long-term assets, or to retire other debts. When a company issues stock, it does not have to repay interest or principal; it sells part of its equity.

In many situations, it is more profitable for the corporation to issue bonds. If future profits will be higher than the interest expense of a bond issue, and if the company can afford repayment, debt capitalization may be chosen over equity.

Bonds are long-term debts, with maturities ranging from a few years to 40 years or more. In this chapter, you will discover the differences between four major classifications of corporate bonds and you will learn about secured debts and unsecured debts; the way a bond issue is offered to the public; how companies use sinking funds to plan ahead for its obligations; methods for retiring bonds; and how to evaluate the risks of buying corporate debt securities.

TYPES OF CORPORATE BONDS

You can purchase mortgage bonds, collateral trust bonds, equipment trust bonds, and debentures issued by corporations. These may be distinguished from one another by the purpose of the debt and by the type of collateral offered by the issuing company.

mortgage bond: a corporate bond secured with the pledge of real property.

When you buy a *mortgage bond*, your position is secured by land or buildings (standing or under construction) owned by the company. In some cases, the bond itself will finance a new office, plant, warehouse, or other facility. In that case, your issue is called a *construction bond* (or completion bond). However, corporations may raise capital through mortgage bonds for any number of reasons.

construction bond: (completion bond) a corporate mortgage bond for property under construction.

collateral trust bond: a corporate bond secured with the pledge of securities held in trust.

When you buy a *collateral trust bond*, it is secured with a portfolio of securities. This portfolio is held in trust, usually at a commercial bank. The issuing company cannot sell those securities until the bond has been retired. Risks to you and to the issuing corporation are reduced when earnings from the portfolio are sufficient to make interest payments. The contract might also specify that the corporation must maintain the collateral value. For example, if a portfolio of stocks falls in market value, the corporation may be required to deposit additional securities in the trust account.

equipment trust bond: a corporate bond issued to purchase capital assets and secured by those assets.

You can also invest in the third classification, *equipment trust bonds*. These are most often associated with transportation companies (airlines, trucking, and railroads) or with oil and gas companies. These industries invest heavily in equipment and machinery and may finance capital acquisitions with bond issues.

Equipment trust bonds are a method of deferred purchase, in which the corporation leases equipment until the bond is retired. The most widely used method of deferred purchase is called the *Philadelphia Plan*. Under this arrangement, the corporation pays 20 percent of the total purchase price and finances the balance with an equipment trust bond issue. An independent trustee is appointed to:

Philadelphia Plan: the most common method for securing collateral for an equipment trust bond. The trustee holds title until the bond has been retired.

- Hold title to the asset until the bond issue has been retired
- Collect lease payments from the corporation
- Supervise care and maintenance of the asset
- Ensure that interest and principal are paid to investors
- Transfer title to the issuer when the entire bond issue has been retired

An alternate method, called the *New York Plan*, is used less frequently. Under this method, the issuing corporation acquires partial title as a bond is gradually retired over a number of years. This is a form of installment purchase, with each installment representing a conditional bill of sale.

New York Plan: an infrequently used method for securing collateral for an equipment trust bond, with purchase made by way of installment purchase.

To purchase capital assets through an equipment trust bond, the company issues a bond with a scheduled series of maturities. These are called *serial bonds*. The total debt is divided into periodic maturities and comes with varying interest rates (based on the years to maturity).

serial bond: a bond issued in periodic segments with varying maturities and interest rates.

official statement:
a summary of a
bond issue's terms:
amount, maturity
date, interest rate,
and trustee.

The terms of the issue are listed in the *official statement*, which identifies the issuing company, issue date, total amount, interest rate and payment dates, and maturity of each serial bond. A sample official statement for an equipment trust bond is shown in Figure 4–1.

This official statement describes a $40 million bond issued in 10 annual maturity installments. While the whole issue is described as a 10.00 percent bond, only those investors who purchase the longer-term installments will be paid that rate. The rate is lower in the earlier years because your interest rate risk is lower. Your capi-

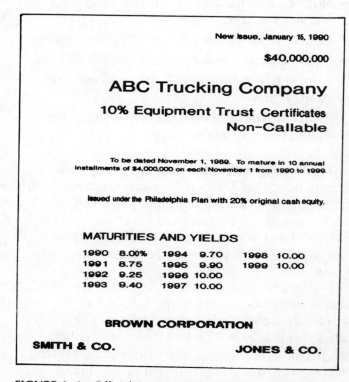

New Issue, January 15, 1990

$40,000,000

ABC Trucking Company

10% Equipment Trust Certificates
Non–Callable

To be dated November 1, 1989. To mature in 10 annual installments of $4,000,000 on each November 1 from 1990 to 1999.

Issued under the Philadelphia Plan with 20% original cash equity.

MATURITIES AND YIELDS

1990	8.00%	1994	9.70	1998	10.00
1991	8.75	1995	9.90	1999	10.00
1992	9.25	1996	10.00		
1993	9.40	1997	10.00		

BROWN CORPORATION

SMITH & CO.   **JONES & CO.**

FIGURE 4–1 Official Statement Describing a Bond Offering

tal will be committed for a relatively short period of time.

The statement also tells you that maturities will occur on November 1 of each year. From this, you can conclude that interest on each installment will be paid on May 1 and on November 1. This is customary for U.S.-issued bonds, but the rule will not necessarily apply on foreign issues. Each serial unit will contain 4,000 bonds, each with a par value of $1,000 (total of $4 million per serial).

Mortgage, collateral trust, and equipment trust bonds are secured by tangible assets. The fourth type of corporate debt, the *debenture*, is unsecured. The corporation pledges only its goodwill and reputation. In the event of default, the debenture is not backed up by the pledge of tangible assets.

debenture: an unsecured corporate debt backed only by goodwill and reputation.

SECURED AND UNSECURED DEBT

You can judge the relative safety of investing in bonds by comparing interest rates, credit ratings, the financial strength and history of the corporation, and whether a bond is secured or unsecured. Among secured bonds, one may not be as safe (or as well secured) as another because it is less senior.

A *"senior"* security is one that will be honored before other obligations. When a bond is described as *junior*, or *subordinated*, that means a previous bond issue will be honored first in the event of default and that the new issue comes next—if funds are available. This applies to both payments of interest and, upon maturity, retirement of the debt. This system defines relative risk of several bonds issued by one com-

senior security: a bond or other debt security with priority of claim in the event of default.

junior security: a bond or other debt security with a subordinated claim in the event of default.

subordination: the assignment of lower priority for one debt in comparison with another.

priority: the sequence in which debts will be honored when the same property is pledged as collateral for different debts.

first mortgage bond: a bond secured by a pledge of real property and holding seniority of claim to that property in the event of default.

general mortgage bond: a bond secured by a pledge of real property with equal or subordinated claim with other creditors in the event of default.

open-end: the status of property pledged as collateral when the priority of claim is equal with the pledge of the same property for other debts.

closed-end: the status of property pledged as collateral when the same property may be pledged for subsequent debts on a subordinated basis.

pany. The *priority* of claim may be of greater significance than the type of collateral backing up a bond.

Debentures, for example, are backed only by the company's promise to repay investors. Debentures are usually subordinated debts, and as an investor, you hold a lower priority of claim that those investors with more senior issues.

The same argument applies to all types of bonds. A mortgage debt, for example, may be issued as a *first mortgage bond* or as a *general mortgage bond*. The first mortgage bond has first claim in the event of default, while a general mortgage bond backed up by the same real property may have junior status. This would become a problem only if the issuing corporation over-pledged one piece of property and then defaulted on its obligations.

Example: You invest in a corporate mortgage bond described as a subordinated debt. This means the real estate pledged as collateral has also been pledged on a previous bond. In the event of default, your claim to the real estate will be honored only after holders of the senior bond issue have been repaid. If equity in the property is adequate, all investors will receive their interest, and principal will be repaid as well; but if the company has overpledged that property, you might receive only part of your original investment or, in an extreme case, none of it.

A bond issued with a tangible asset pledged as collateral may be *open-end* or *closed-end*. Under an open-end commitment, one asset can be pledged as collateral for additional debts, and all creditors will have equal claim in the event of default. Under a closed-end agreement, the same property may be pledged as collateral on subsequent debts, but those creditors will have a junior claim; their debt will be subordinate to the claims of the first creditors.

THE PUBLIC OFFERING

When a corporation issues a bond, many players become involved. The "official statement," also called a "tombstone," is published in a financial newspaper and announces only the highlights. To get the bond to the buyer, the corporation must go through several steps (listed below), comply with filing and disclosure requirements, and employ the services of groups that can reach the market and sell the bond to you and other investors.

The steps in a public offering are:

1. The corporation's board of directors makes the decision to raise capital through a bond issue.

2. The company retains an *investment banker*, usually a securities broker-dealer, to underwrite the bond issue. A single investment banker or a consolidation of two or more will become the lead *underwriter* for the bond offering.

The investment banker may be retained to participate in one of two ways. When acting *as principal*, the investment banker purchases the entire bond issue from the corporation and then offers it to the public. Or the investment banker may act *as agent*, in which case it promises to market as much of the issue as possible. This arrangement is called a "best efforts" agreement.

3. The new offering must be registered with the *Securities and Exchange Commission* (SEC). The SEC, the primary regulatory agency for the

investment banker: a securities broker-dealer or other firm that organizes the marketing activities for the public offering of a bond.

underwriter: the combination of companies that places a bond on the market, including the lead underwriter (investment banker) and the selling group.

as principal: the status of an investment banker who purchases an entire bond issue and then resells units to investors.

as agent: the status of an investment banker who promises to market as much of the issue as possible (a "best efforts" agreement).

Securities and Exchange Commission (SEC): an organization that regulates the securities industry, created by provisions of the Securities and Exchange Act of 1934.

registration statement: a disclosure document the issuer is required to file with the Securities and Exchange Commission (SEC) for a bond issue. The statement describes the terms of the bond, including collateral pledged, maturity date, interest rate and payment dates, and the trustee's name and address.

cooling-off period: a period between filing of a bond's registration statement and the first date the issue may be offered to the public. This period is normally 20 days.

preliminary prospectus (red herring): a document similar to the registration statement, but intended for investors who may want to file an indication of interest. It is called a "red herring" because disclosures made on the front page are in bright red ink.

securities industry, was created under the terms of the Securities and Exchange Act of 1934 and today regulates the industry and the individuals working in it. A new offering *registration statement* describes all of the terms of the issue.

4. The actual offering can be made to the public 20 days after filing the registration. (In some cases, permission is given to offer the bond before this date.) The 20 days are referred to as the *"cooling-off period."*

5. The issuing corporation issues a *preliminary prospectus* (also called a "red herring" because of the red lettering on the cover disclosing the terms and risks of the offering). The underwriter is not allowed to solicit orders for the bond until the cooling-off period has expired. However, the underwriter may distribute the preliminary prospectus to obtain *"indications of interest"* from investors.

6. The *final prospectus* is prepared and given to investors. This document discloses all of the information given to the SEC through the registration statement that investors need to make an informed decision, including the amount of the issue, offering price, maturity date, interest rate and payment dates, collateral, seniority, and other disclosures. Disclosure and the prospectus are mandatory under terms of the Securities Act of 1933.

7. The issuing company prepares an *indenture* for the bond. The indenture is the contract between the issuer (corporation) and the creditor (investor). The form and content of this document are dictated by the terms of the Trust Indenture Act of 1939. Disclosure must include:

- The interest rate and payment dates
- The maturity date
- Conditions for repayment prior to maturity, if applicable

- A complete description of collateral, including level of seniority
- The name and address of the trustee

THE UNDERWRITER'S ROLE

The issuer and trustee are responsible for preparing the documents required by law and for disclosing all of the elements and conditions of the bond issue. At the same time, the investment banker is responsible for organizing a group of companies to sell the issue.

As the lead underwriter, the investment banker forms an underwriting *syndicate*—a group of companies that will share the underwriting responsibility. The lead underwriter will probably be one of the companies in the syndicate. Next, a *selling group* comprised of several securities broker-dealers is formed. This group will sell the bonds directly to the buyers.

Bonds are sold directly by the underwriting/ selling group to institutional investors—mutual funds, pension plans, insurance companies, banks, savings and loans. Individuals may also purchase one or more bonds directly through their brokers. The organization of a public offering is shown in Figure 4–2.

SINKING FUNDS

The issuing corporation must plan for repayment of its investors. The typical bond can be compared to an interest-only loan with a balloon payment at the end of the term. As many homeowners have discovered, without planning, balloon payments can be difficult to make. With

indications of interest: tentative reservations of bond units made by investors prior to expiration of the cooling-off period.

final prospectus: the full disclosure document that must be given to all investors in newly issued bonds, required by terms of the Securities Act of 1933. The prospectus explains the amount of the issue, maturity date, interest rate and payment dates, the trustee's name and address, and the type of collateral.

indenture: the agreement entered between the corporation (issuer) and the investor (creditor). All terms of the agreement are specified, including the total of the bond issue, maturity date, interest rate and payment dates, and the trustee's name and address.

syndicate: the organizations that

will jointly under-write a bond issue, representing the corporation and working through a selling group.

selling group: the broker-dealers who sell bonds to inves-tors, contracted by the underwriting syndicate.

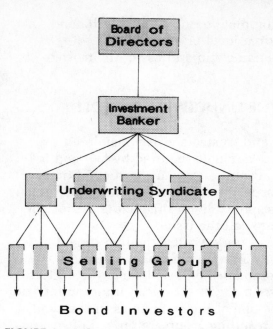

FIGURE 4–2 Organization of a Public Bond Offering

sinking fund: a re-serve account es-tablished to accumulate funds to retire a future debt. A periodic payment to the fund, plus earn-ings, is calculated to produce the re-quired maturity value of bond is-sues.

that problem in mind, the corporation may establish a special reserve account called a *sinking fund*, so that the money will be available to retire a bond in the future. The company deposits money periodically (monthly, quarterly, or annually) so that by maturity date, the balance of deposits, plus earnings, will be on hand to pay investors and retire the bond issue.

Example: A corporation has a bond issue outstanding with a redemption value of $3 million. It sets up a sinking fund and makes payments at the end of each year to save the money it will need in 20 years. The fixed interest rate on the account is 7 percent (compounded annually).

To determine how much must be deposited at the end of each year, the company refers to a compound interest table called "Sinking

Fund Factors." This table shows a factor for the amount necessary at the end of each period to accumulate the required fund.

The table for 7 percent (with interest compounded annually) shows a 20-year factor of 0.0243929. To figure out what annual deposit is required, multiply the factor by the target amount:

$$0.0243929 \times \$3{,}000{,}000 = \$73{,}178.70$$

Rounded to the nearest dollar, the amount the company must deposit per year to accumulate $3 million in 20 years is $73,179.

The 20-year outcome is summarized in Table 4–A. Each year's ending balance is multiplied by .07 (the decimal equivalent of 7 percent); the interest is added to the previous balance and to the additional yearly deposit.

A book of compound interest tables will provide factors for sinking funds, usually at half-percent or quarter-percent points. To compute the amount of deposit required for interest rates not found in a book of tables, use the sinking fund formula shown in Figure 4–3.

This formula can be applied to the example above to prove that it produces the needed amount of periodic deposits:

$$D = \$3{,}000{,}000 \left[\frac{1}{(\,(1 + .07)^{20} - 1) \,/\, .07} \right]$$

$$= \$3{,}000{,}000 \left[\frac{1}{(3.86968 - 1) \,/\, .07} \right]$$

$$= \$3{,}000{,}000 \left[\frac{1}{40.99543} \right]$$

$$= \$3{,}000{,}000 \, [.0243929]$$

$$= \$73{,}178.70$$

TABLE 4–A Yearly Deposits Required for a 20-Year Sinking Fund

Year	Deposit	7% Interest	Balance
1	$73,179	$ 0	$ 73,179
2	73,179	5,123	151,481
3	73,179	10,603	235,263
4	73,179	16,469	324,911
5	73,179	22,743	420,833
6	73,179	29,459	523,471
7	73,179	36,643	633,293
8	73,179	44,330	750,802
9	73,179	52,556	876,537
10	73,179	61,358	1,011,074
11	73,179	70,775	1,155,028
12	73,179	80,852	1,309,059
13	73,179	91,634	1,473,872
14	73,179	103,172	1,650,223
15	73,179	115,515	1,838,917
16	73,179	128,724	2,040,820
17	73,179	142,856	2,256,855
18	73,179	157,981	2,488,015
19	73,179	174,163	2,735,357
20	73,179	191,473	3,000,009

$$D = A \left[\frac{1}{((1 + r)^n - 1) + r} \right]$$

D = deposit amount
A = target amount
r = interest rate
n = number of periods

FIGURE 4–3 Formula for Required Periodic Deposits in a Sinking Fund

RETIRING THE BOND

Bonds have a finite life—they are designed for redemption at a specified date in the future. Stocks, in comparison, can be held for as short or as long a period as you desire. The most obvious method of retiring a bond is according to the terms of the indenture: At maturity date, you are paid the par value of the bond. The corporation may set up a sinking fund in order to honor its obligation, or it may employ a number of other options to achieve full retirement.

One method is called _refunding_. The corporation replaces an older bond issue with a newer one, thus deferring the retirement of the debt. Refunding may also replace a previous bond's interest rate with a new, lower one.

Another method of retiring a bond is through _open-market purchase_. The corporation buys and then cancels its own bonds at the then prevailing market price. This is most likely to occur when the corporation has funds available and when bonds are selling at a discount. The difference between the discounted value and the par value represents a profit, since the issuer pays less than the full amount of obligation on its debt.

The reason for open-market purchase of a debt is similar to that for a company's purchase of its own stock. Corporations may retire equity by buying shares on the open market, creating Treasury stock. By doing this, the company reduces future dividend payments.

Another way to retire a bond is through exercise of a _call feature_. Some bonds are issued with the understanding that the issuer has the right to retire the debt before the maturity date, or to "call up" the bond. The issuer may retire

refunding: one method of retiring a bond issue, in which previous bonds are replaced with newly issued ones.

open-market purchase: one method of retiring all or part of a bond issue in which the corporation purchases its own bonds on the open market at current market price.

call feature: a feature written into some bond indentures giving the issuer the right to redeem all or part of the issue prior to scheduled maturity date.

callable bond: a bond containing a call feature.

call protection: the period of time between issue date and the first possible call date.

all or part of the debt, and specific call dates are usually spelled out in the indenture.

Callable bonds are issued with a degree of *call protection*. This is the time between issue date and the first call date. Calling a bond is advantageous to the corporation when current market interest rates are lower than the bond rate. The call is comparable to a homeowner's decision to refinance a mortgage debt because current interest rates are lower.

The bond issuer has a contractual obligation to pay the investor (creditor) upon maturity or to satisfy the debt by refunding, open-market purchase, or call. The bondholder, in comparison, may close the investment position by selling the bond on the open market exchange.

Another choice is available for convertible bonds, that is, bonds that can be exchanged for a specified number of shares of common stock. With a convertible bond, your debt position can be transferred into an equity position. You would want to make the conversion when the potential profit from stock ownership is greater than the realized profit from the bond, considering interest versus dividend as well as current market value. Conversion is explained in more detail in Chapter 8.

EVALUATING RISKS

Collateral defines the degree of risk in a particular bond. For example, a collateral trust bond is issued by a corporation that is very strong financially, and it is backed with a conservative portfolio in which minimum value adequate to retire the entire issue must be maintained. For these reasons, the yield on this bond is on the low side. A subordinated debenture, on the other hand, is issued by a corporation whose financial strength is marginal and whose debt capitalization has been growing during recent years as equity has declined. The yield on this bond is much higher, but so are the risks of default of both interest and principal.

Several events may occur when a corporation defaults on a bond. The choice the issuer faces is to liquidate assets to satisfy the obligation or to reorganize. Upon reorganization, interest payments or even the maturity date may be suspended.

One of the terms of an income bond is that interest will be paid only if and when the corporation can afford it. Interest accrues each year if payments are missed. If the company is in serious trouble, you might never receive interest payments, and you could lose your entire investment.

In that case, you will have an investment worth more on paper but worthless in reality. Income bonds may give you the only chance, however remote, of getting back something from your investment in the future. The alternative—a complete default of the issuing corporation—is worse, because in that case, you may get nothing. When a company is financially distressed, a delay in payment of its debts can provide the relief needed to return to a profitable stance and, ultimately, to pay its creditors.

Default is not the only risk you face. Another type of risk is that your funds will be committed for many years, and at a rate of interest that is low by comparison with future market rates. A bond with 30 years to maturity might trade at a deep discount for several years, so that you would be unable to get your capital back with-

out absorbing a capital loss. By contrast, a bond
with only a few years until maturity represents
less risk. Long-term bonds represent a time risk
as well, since you have no way of knowing future interest rates. The longer the term, the more
uncertain whether today's yield is relatively
high or low. A 30-year commitment could involve an opportunity risk. Your evaluation
should be based on comparisons of yield to maturity, the time until maturity, current market
price, and safety rating (see Chapter 9). Also
compare the risks of investing in corporate
bonds with those associated with other choices,
such as U.S. government securities. That is the
subject of the next chapter.

5

U.S. Government Securities

The U.S. government and its departments and agencies issue a large number of debt securities. Just as corporations borrow money to finance expansion and operations through debt instruments, the government borrows money to pay its expenses.

The national debt is financed through Treasury bills, notes, and bonds; savings bonds; and other short-term and long-term instruments. Projects sponsored by government agencies are financed with bonds, and two major capital needs—farm and home financing—represent most of the bond issue volume in government-sponsored agencies.

FEATURES OF GOVERNMENT SECURITIES

Several important features distinguish U.S. goverment debt securities from the corporate vari-

original-issue discount: the method under which most U.S. government securities are issued. Investors buy debt securities at a discount and accrue interest during the holding period. Upon maturity, the investor receives par value.

marketable security: a security that is traded publicly, directly with other investors through the exchange market.

nonmarketable security: a government debt security that cannot be traded publicly, but must be purchased and redeemed through the Federal Reserve system or through the U.S. Treasury.

ety. The most important feature is called the "full faith and credit guarantee"—a pledge by the government to repay its direct obligations. Because the government has the power to assess and collect taxes, the guarantee makes these securities virtually free of risk.

While government securities are often described as "risk-free," you should be aware that there are various forms of risk. There is virtually no risk of default when you buy a Treasury debt instrument, but other risks may affect your decision.

One of these risks is that the interest rate you receive from government securities may be lower than what you could earn on corporate bonds. However, considering the default and liquidity risks associated with corporates, the lower interest rate may be justified, especially when you diversify your portfolio.

Many U.S. government securities are sold at a discount from face value and accrue interest from issue date to maturity date. This arrangement is called *original-issue discount*. The current market value of the bond is determined by accrued interest and time the instrument is held, and not by changing interest rates and market demand. You might consider this an advantage if you are using government debt securities to save for retirement or a child's college education. Or you may see it as a disadvantage considering the capital gains you could earn by investing in other debt securities.

Some government securities are *marketable*, meaning that they can be traded publicly and will vary in value based on demand and interest rates. These include Treasury bills, notes, and bonds. Other government securities are *nonmarketable*, meaning they are registered to the origi-

nal owner and cannot be bought or sold on the
open market. They are purchased and redeemed
through the Federal Reserve system or the U.S.
Treasury only. For example, Series EE and HH
savings bonds cannot be transferred. The original owner must redeem them through a savings
institution or through the U.S. Treasury.

Another feature of the most common Treasury
securities is that they are exempt from state and
local taxes. This rule applies to Treasury bills,
notes, and bonds, as well as to Series EE and HH
bonds. However, all of these investments are
taxed at the federal level.

Treasury securities can provide another tax
benefit. The interest on certain discounted bonds
is often not taxable until those bonds mature.
And with some instruments, such as Series EE
bonds, you have the option of paying tax on
earnings each year or deferring payment until
maturity. The exemption from state and local
taxes could make the yield from government securities more attractive than the yield from a
very safe corporate bond with a higher rate of interest.

Yet another feature that makes government
debt securities attractive is the lack of a sales
charge when they are purchased directly from
the Treasury. You do not pay a fee for buying or
selling securities, and there is no management
fee, commission, or other assessment. Depending
on the method you use to invest in corporate or
municipal bonds, this advantage should be included in the comparison of net yield.

BILLS, NOTES, AND BONDS

The U.S. government sells debt securities to
fund its programs, pay salaries and other operat-

ing expenses, and meet its obligations. Investors are repaid from future tax revenues. The amount of debt the government needs to sell each year is determined by the federal budget, which includes debt service (the payment of obligations to existing investors). The amount of public debt increases whenever payments exceed revenues (which derive primarily from taxes).

Most of the volume in public debt takes place through three instruments: bills, notes, and bonds. These are distinguished by several features, including discount at issue, denomination size, maturity, timing of sale or auction, interest rate, timing of earnings, and taxation, which are summarized in Figure 5–1.

Treasury bill: a short-term U.S. government debt with maturities of 13, 26, or 52 weeks. Minimum denomination is $10,000.

1. *Treasury bills (T-bills).* T-bills are always sold at a discount, in denominations of $10,000 and with multiples of $5,000 above that level. They mature in 13, 26, or 52 weeks. Because maturity always occurs in one year or less, T-bills are the federal government version of money market instruments. (The money market deals in debt obligations with maturities of one year or less, while the capital market includes instruments maturing beyond one year.)

Treasury bills are sold every Monday (for 13- and 26-week maturities) or every four weeks (for 52-week maturities). The interest rate you will earn on a T-bill investment is not announced ahead of time because the rate is set in a competitive bid auction. Interest is realized upon sale or maturity of the bill.

Treasury note: a U.S. government debt maturing between 2 and 10 years from issue date. Denominations are $1,000, $5,000, $10,000, $100,000, and $1 million.

2. *Treasury notes.* Notes are available in denominations of $1,000, $5,000, $10,000, $100,000, and $1 million. Maturities vary with each note, from 2 to 10 years, and new issues are marketed according to an auction calendar,

	BILLS	NOTES	BONDS
ISSUE FORM	always discounted	usually discounted	
DENOMINATION	$10,000 minimum and multiples of $5,000	$1,000, $5,000, $10,000 and $1 million	$1,000, $5,000, $10,000, $100,000 and $1 million
MATURITY	13, 26, or 52 weeks	2 to 10 years	over 10 years
SOLD	every Monday (13– and 26–week); every 4 weeks (52–week)	usually once per month	usually in February, May, August and November
INTEREST RATE	determined by competitive bid auction		
INTEREST EARNED	when sold or matured	earned each year	
TAXES	exempt from state and local taxes; taxable at federal level		

FIGURE 5–1 Comparison of U.S. Government Securities

Treasury bond: a U.S. government debt maturing beyond 10 years from issue date. Denominations are $1,000, $5,000, $10,000, $100,000, and $1 million.

approximately once per month. Interest rates are determined by competitive bid auction, and interest is paid semiannually.

3. *Treasury bonds.* Bonds are sold in denominations of $1,000, $5,000, $10,000, $100,000, and $1 million. They mature in more than 10 years.

Competitive bid auctions are announced four times per year, in February, May, August, and November. Interest is paid semiannually.

COST AND YIELD

You will need to figure out the actual cost of a discounted Treasury security and determine the annual yield in order to make a comparison with other investment alternatives. To perform the necessary calculations, you need to know several things:

1. *The asked discount.* This is the percentage of discount at which a dealer is willing to sell a Treasury security. In Treasury security quotations, the asked discount is expressed as a percentage. For example, when the asked discount is listed as 5.95, that means you will be buying the debt instrument at a discount of 5.95 percent.

2. *Days to maturity.* The calculation also depends on the number of days between purchase and maturity dates. For example, if you purchase a T-bill on January 5 and it matures on January 28, there are 23 days to maturity.

3. *Par value.* To find the current market price, you need to know how much you will receive upon maturity—the par, or face, value. The computation of today's market price is based on a 360-day year and assumes that every month has 30 days. Market price is equal to:

$$\text{Par value} - \frac{(\text{Par value} \times \text{asked discount} \times \text{days})}{360}$$

Example: You are reviewing a T-bill with a par value of $10,000 on January 5. It matures on January 28, in 23 days, and the current asked discount is listed as 5.95. To compute market price:

$$= 10,000 - \frac{(10,000 \times .0595 \times 23)}{360}$$

$$= 10,000 - \frac{13,685}{360}$$

$$= 10,000 - 38.01$$

$$= 9,961.99$$

You would pay $9,961.99 today for this T-bill. In 23 days, you would be paid the par value of $10,000. The difference, $38.01, is profit representing 5.95 percent—based on the par value of $10,000. The formula for computing the market price of a discounted security is summarized in Figure 5–2.

$$P - \left[\frac{P \times A \times D}{360} \right] = M$$

P = par value
A = asked discount
D = days to maturity
M = market price

FIGURE 5–2 Formula for the Market Price of a Discounted Security

This formula can be proven by annualizing the yield:

Step 1: Divide the amount of interest by the par value:

$$\frac{38.01}{10,000} = .003801$$

Step 2: Divide the answer by 23 (days):

$$\frac{.003801}{23} = .0001652$$

Step 3: Multiply the answer by 360 days:

$$.0001652 \times 360 = .059472$$

Rounded out, this equals .0595, the decimal equivalent of 5.95 percent.

These steps prove the calculation, but only for the purpose of determining market price. For two reasons, the true annualized yield will be different. First, the yield must be based on the actual amount you invest and not on the par value. Second, annualized yield is based on a 365-day year, not on the 360-day year used to set a discounted price.

Annualized yield is equal to:

$$\frac{(\text{par value} - \text{market price}) \times 365}{\text{days} \times \text{market price}}$$

Applying this formula to our example, the par value is $10,000 and the market price is $9,961.99. There are 23 days to maturity. The annualized yield formula:

$$= \frac{(10,000 - 9,961.99) \times 365}{23 \times 9,961.99}$$

$$= \frac{13,873.65}{229,125.77}$$

$$= 6.06\%$$

The annualized yield in this example is 6.06 percent. The formula is summarized in Figure 5–3.

An alternative method is *discount yield*, also called *equivalent bond yield*. In this case, yield is based on par value rather than on the amount invested (discount). Discount yield is figured in this way:

$$\frac{\text{Discount}}{\text{Par value}} \times \frac{365}{\text{Days to maturity}}$$

discount yield (equivalent bond yield): a method of computing the yield on Treasury securities based on par value rather than on the discounted purchase price.

Using the same example applied to compute annualized yield, in which par value is $10,000, the discount amount is $38.01, and there are 23 days to maturity, discount yield is:

$$\frac{38.01}{10,000} \times \frac{365}{23} = .0603$$

The answer, .0603, is the decimal equivalent of 6.03 percent, the discount yield. The formula is summarized in Figure 5–4.

$$\frac{(P - M) \times 365}{D \times M} = Y$$

P = par value
M = market price
D = days to maturity
Y = annualized yield

FIGURE 5–3 Formula for Annualized Yield of a Discounted Security

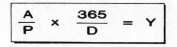

A = amount of discount
P = par value
D = days to maturity
Y = discount yield

FIGURE 5–4 Formula for Discount Yield

U.S. SAVINGS BONDS

Treasury bills, notes, and bonds are the marketable forms of U.S. government securities. Savings bonds, in comparison, are nonmarketable. They can be purchased only from the Treasury (usually through a savings institution) and can only be redeemed in the same manner. There are two types of savings bonds available today.

Series EE Bonds

Series EE bonds are sold in discounted form and mature in approximately 9½ years. The actual maturity will vary based on interest rates, which are adjusted every six months.

The rate paid on Series EE bonds held five years or more is equal to 85 percent of the average yield on other Treasury securities. The minimum guaranteed rate is 7½ percent.

You can cash in a Series EE bond at any time after a holding period of six months. (They can be cashed in earlier in the event of emergency.) You will never receive less than the amount invested, which is one-half the maturity value. Denominations are $50, $75, $100, $200, $500, $1,000, $5,000, and $10,000. Purchase price of

Series EE bond: a U.S. government security issued at one-half par value, available in denominations of $50, $75, $100, $200, $500, $1,000, $5,000, and $10,000. The bond is nontransferrable and cannot be pledged as collateral. Minimum guaranteed interest is 7½ percent. Bonds held five years or more yield 85 percent of the average yield on other Treasury securities.

each bond is one-half the denomination level. For example, a $50 bond is purchased for $25.

Interest is not paid, but accrued during the holding period. At maturity, the Series EE bond will be worth par value (or more). The bond can be held beyond the maturity date, and interest will continue to accrue.

Series EE bonds are exempt from state and local taxes, but are taxed at the federal level. You have a choice of paying tax on a portion of the gain earned each year or waiting until your EE bond matures and is cashed in. At that point, all of the income is taxable. Another choice is to exchange Series EE bonds for Series HH bonds. In that case, tax on EE bond earnings is deferred for the time you own the HH bond, but income from the HH bond is taxed each year.

Each individual is limited to an annual $30,000 in face value per year in Series EE bonds. However, a husband and wife may each purchase up to this limit.

Series HH Bonds

You can purchase _Series HH bonds_ in only one way: by exchanging Series EE bonds with a current market value of $500 or more. The HH bond matures in 10 years. Interest is paid every six months and is taxed in the year paid.

Both Series EE and Series HH bonds are registered in the name of the original purchaser, and ownership cannot be transferred. And because they are nontransferrable, these bonds cannot be used as collateral.

If certificates are lost or stolen, the Treasury will replace them free of charge. (See the address at the end of this chapter to request a replacement certificate.) It is a good idea to write

Series HH bond: a U.S. government security that is purchased only by exchanging Series EE bonds with current market value of $500 or more. Maturity is 10 years, and interest is paid twice per year.

down the purchase and denomination amount, date of purchase, and bond serial number for each purchase, and to keep the list separate from the certificates. If you do need to ask for a replacement, having this information will speed up the process.

Savings bonds can be used for a number of financial goals. Because they are very safe and come with a guaranteed minimum interest rate, their future value is dependable. Buying Series EE bonds each month is one method of accumulating funds for college education, future mortgage payments, or retirement.

The fact that savings bonds are nonmarketable may be inconvenient, but it also protects your investment. No one else can cash a stolen Series EE or Series HH bond because they are registered in your name and cannot be pledged, assigned, or transferred.

GOVERNMENT AGENCY BONDS

A number of agencies of the federal government, and corporations supervised by agencies, issue bonds, both directly and in pools similar to mutual funds. Some of these bonds are guaranteed by the full faith and credit of the U.S. government, and others are not. When comparing bonds for safety features, be sure that you understand relative degrees of risk.

Agency bonds are issued in two primary areas: farming and housing. The agencies lend money to individuals, associations, and corporations for specific reasons and finance those loans through bond issues.

Farm Credit System Securities

Three separate agencies lend money for farming activities, and their bonds are sold through the Federal Farm Credit Funding Corporation in New York. All three agencies are jointly liable for debt securities issued. Even though they are not federal agencies, the three agencies are supervised by the Farm Credit Administration. They are:

1. Bank for Cooperatives—This agency was created under provisions of the Farm Credit Act of 1933 to finance farm association and cooperative operations. The federal government originally owned and controlled the agency, which was converted to private ownership under terms of the Farm Credit Act of 1955.

2. Federal Intermediate Credit Banks—This agency was formed as part of the Agricultural Credits Act of 1923 to provide funds to lenders who finance farm activities. Today, FICB is privately owned, as mandated by terms of the Farm Credit Act of 1956.

3. Federal Land Bank—This agency was created under terms of the Federal Farm Loan Act of 1916, and like the other agencies in the system, it is privately owned today. The FLB grants secured first mortgage loans on farm properties.

Bonds of all three agencies are exempt from state and local taxes and are taxed at the federal level. None of these loans is guaranteed by the full faith and credit of the U.S. government. However, they are backed by the assets of participating federally chartered savings and loan and banking institutions.

Mortgage Credit Agencies

The second major group of federal agencies specializes in financing home ownership. These agencies include:

1. Federal Home Loan Bank—This agency was created under terms of the Federal Home Loan Bank Act of 1932. It oversees lending activities of federally chartered savings and loan associations, banks, insurance companies, and other institutions in the home mortgage business.

2. Federal National Mortgage Association—Also known by the acronym "Fannie Mae," this company was created as part of the National Housing Act of 1938. The FNMA provides a secondary market for mortgages insured by the Federal Housing Administration. The agency is supervised by the Department of Housing and Urban Development.

3. Government National Mortgage Association—Also known by the acronym "Ginnie Mae," this agency is an offshoot of the FNMA. It was created by terms of the Housing and Urban Development Act of 1968. FNMA became a privately owned corporation under the 1968 act, while GNMA was created as a government-owned company. GNMA buys mortgages guaranteed by the Veterans Administration or insured by the Federal Housing Administration. It creates mortgage pools (like mutual funds made up from a number of home mortgages) and sells shares to investors.

Interest on bonds or mortgage pool shares issued by all three mortgage credit agencies is exempt from state and local taxes and subject to federal income tax. GNMA bonds and pool shares are guaranteed by the full faith and credit of the U.S. government.

Other federal agencies, in addition to the farm and housing groups that represent most of this market, issue bonds. They include the Export–Import Bank, the Tennessee Valley Authority, the U.S. Postal Service, and the Student Loan Marketing Association (also known as "Sallie Mae").

INFORMATION SOURCES

The Treasury Department and the Federal Reserve banks provide a number of free brochures and other information useful to anyone considering investing in U.S. government securities:

Public Debt Information
U.S. Department of the Treasury
Washington DC 20226

Write for two brochures: "Information About Treasury Notes and Bonds" and "Information About Treasury Bills."

Federal Reserve Bank of Dallas
Public Affairs Department
Station K
Dallas TX 75222

Ask for the booklet "United States Treasury Securities: Basic Information."

Federal Reserve Bank of Richmond
Bank and Public Relations Department
Box 2762
Richmond VA 23262

Write and request "Buying Treasury Securities at Federal Reserve Banks."

Federal Reserve Bank of New York
Public Information Department
33 Liberty Street
New York NY 10045

Send for the booklet "Basic Information on Treasury Bills."

Investors in Series EE bonds can find out the current rate being paid by calling a toll-free number, 1-800-USBONDS. Savings bond investors whose certificates are lost or stolen can request replacements by writing to:

Bureau of Public Debt
Parkersburg WV 26106-1328

Include the purchase date, denomination, and serial number of lost certificates, if you have this information.

Investors can determine the current market value of savings bonds by writing to:

Office of Public Affairs
U.S. Savings Bond Division
Department of the Treasury
Washington DC 20226

Ask for table PD 3600. This will list the current market value for your savings bonds.

The federal government is not the only government that pays its expenses through debt securities. States, counties, cities, and other municipalities also offer bonds and notes to investors. That is the subject of the next chapter.

6

Municipal Debt Securities

You help finance the construction of highways, schools, dams, power plants, sports stadiums, and any number of other facilities when you invest in municipal bonds and notes. Any governmental body, agency, or subdivision not part of the federal government is classified as a municipality, and its debts are municipal bonds.

These bonds are issued by states, territories, possessions, counties, cities, townships, or political subdivisions of states or territories. In most cases, they are issued in $5,000 units and in bearer form, meaning that the individual in possession of the bond certificate is assumed to be the owner.

Although securities, in general, are regulated by the Securities and Exchange Commission, the municipal bond industry was not directly regulated until 1975, when the Securities Act Amendment of 1975 created the Municipal Securities Rulemaking Board (MSRB), which serves as a self-regulatory agency. The MSRB has established rules of fair practice and operating and reporting procedures. Municipal issues must be registered with the MSRB, just as other securities are registered with the Securities and Exchange Commission.

Historically, "muni" bonds have proven, for the most part, to be fairly safe investments. During the Depression of the 1930s, less than 2 percent of all municipal issues defaulted, and most of those eventually paid accrued interest and investors' principal.

The existence of the MSRB does not ensure that your investment is completely safe. Muni bonds are *not* as safe as U.S. government securities. Some notable defaults have occurred in recent history. In 1974, the Washington Public Power Supply System had a $2.05 billion default. In 1987, 123 issues with a total value of $1.1 billion were defaulted. In 1988, 129 issues with a total value of $944.6 million went into default. And in the first half of 1989, 33 issues with a total value of $435.8 million were defaulted.[1]

The safety of a municipal bond investment will depend on the rating assigned to the issuer (see Chapter 9, "Information Sources") and on the type of bond that is involved. While muni bonds come in a number of varieties, and proceeds are used to finance a number of projects, they can be broadly put into two groups: general obligation and revenue bonds.

MAJOR TYPES OF MUNICIPAL DEBT

Municipalities issue both General Obligation and Revenue bonds. Corporations collateralize many

---

[1]Statistics cited in "A Warning on Muni Bonds," *Changing Times* magazine, August 1989.

of their bonds with real estate or a portfolio of securities. But municipal bond issues are not backed by a tangible asset in the same manner. A *general obligation* (GO) *bond* is pledged by the taxing power of the issuer. The GO bond is also called a "full faith and credit" bond.

Taxing power is not absolute at any level. The U.S. government has greater taxing power than the states, and the states generally have more taxing power than counties or cities. The state may pledge income, excise, sales, and other taxes as security for its bonds. Counties and cities, though, are generally limited to property taxes, which means that their power is finite. They cannot pledge security beyond the future taxes that will be collectible from their citizens. To incur debt beyond that level, the county or city must seek a special assessment, usually meaning the voters must approve the decision.

GOs can be limited or unlimited. A *limited tax bond* is restricted by the issuer's existing taxing power, and additional taxes cannot be enacted to meet the obligation. An *unlimited tax bond* is one for which the issuer is authorized to raise taxes or incur new taxes, if needed, to meet the debt obligation.

The second category of municipal debt is *revenue bonds*. These are usually issued by an agency, authority, or district of a municipality. Proceeds are used to build facilities, such as terminals, ports, utility plants, dams, bridges, hospitals, and schools.

Because the issuer is an agency of a municipality, the bond is not guaranteed directly. Payment is pledged from future revenues, but that does not ensure that future revenue will be sufficient to repay the interest and principal invested by bondholders. Thus, revenue bonds are con-

general obligation bond: a municipal bond secured by the taxing power of the issuer, also called a full faith and credit bond.

limited tax bond: a general obligation bond restricted by the issuer's taxing power. Additional taxes may not be raised to meet the obligation.

unlimited tax bond: a general obligation bond not restricted by the issuer's current taxing power. The issuer has the right to raise additional taxes, if necessary, to meet the bond obligation.

revenue bond: a municipal bond issued by an agency, authority, or district and secured by future revenues derived from operation of a facility.

sidered higher risks than general obligation bonds.

In some cases, the municipality will assume responsibility for repayment of the bond debt. If so, a revenue bond takes on the features of a general obligation bond—a hybrid form. In other instances, the revenue bond is secured by future revenues, but the issuer promises to repay investors even if revenues are not adequate. When this occurs, the debt is called a *moral obligation bond*. However, while the issuer may honor its pledge, it is not legally bound by it. The debt is still secured only by future revenues.

moral obligation bond: a bond issued with a promise to make repayment even if revenue is insufficient.

Revenue bonds are issued to finance construction of facilities for a wide range of purposes, and they are repaid from future taxes. One variation is the special tax or assessment bond, which is secured by a temporary tax or by a one-time assessment. The tax may be directly related to the project—for example, an increase in the gasoline tax used to construct a pollution treatment plant. Or it may be unrelated—for example, retail sales taxes increased to finance a highway improvement or expansion project.

Short-term municipal debts are classified as notes. They are usually sold at discount, with interest accrued from issue date to maturity. In comparison, bonds are usually sold at or near par, with interest paid twice per year.

There are three types of municipal notes:

tax anticipation note (TAN): a mortgage note pledged by taxes to be received in the near future.

1. *Tax anticipation note (TAN).* The TAN is issued to provide immediate funds for operation of the municipality and is secured by tax revenues that will be received in the near future.

Example: A county expects to receive a property tax installment on October 31, representing the first half-payment for the year beginning in July. On July 1, the county issues a TAN to fund its budgeted operations for the next four months. The debt will be repaid from taxes collected by October 31.

2. *Revenue anticipation note (RAN).* The proceeds from a RAN are used to pay the operating costs of a facility or to pay for the completion of a facility or project. These debts are secured by revenues to be received in the near future.

revenue anticipation note (RAN): a mortgage note pledged by future project or facility revenues.

Example: A port authority is nearing completion of a newly constructed shipping terminal. During the next six months, operating costs will be incurred but revenues will be minimal. The authority issues a six-month RAN to fund operating expenses, secured by revenues it will receive by the end of the period.

3. *Bond anticipation note (BAN).* The BAN provides temporary financing to the municipality when proceeds from a bond issue are pending and will be received in the near future.

bond anticipation note (BAN): a mortgage note pledged by future bond proceeds.

Example: A municipality is in the process of marketing a major bond offering to construct a new school. Proceeds will be received within the next six months, but the municipality wants to begin construction immediately. A BAN is sold to begin the project, and it will be repaid once the bond goes on the market.

THE BOND INDENTURE

Muni bonds, like corporates, are issued as open-end or closed-end debt obligations. Under the open-end arrangement, the issuer can incur additional debts that contain an identical pledge, and all bondholders will have equal claim to pledged tax or revenue—no one issue will be senior to another. Under a closed-end issue, no equal-claim financing is allowed. If additional bonds are issued, they will have junior claims to the original bondholders' debt.

The major terms of the indenture (contract) are described in the official statement and highlighted on the cover of that statement. A sample of the cover is shown in Figure 6–1. In this sample, the Metropolitan Transportation Authority has declared a new issue that includes three types of bonds: serial, term, and zero coupon.

The official statement's cover includes all of the terms of the issue. The detailed explanations below correspond to the numbered items in the figure.

1. *Total amount of the issue.* The total is $382,270,000, which will be used to finance transit facility and commuter facility services.

2. *Name of authority issuing the bond.* The Metropolitan Transportation Authority is the issuer.

dated date (issue date): the date when interest begins to accrue on a newly issued bond.

3. *Issue and maturity date.* The "*dated date*" (issue date) is the date that bond obligations are sold to investors. Upon that date, interest accrual begins. This section also shows that each bond in the issue will mature on July 1 of the applicable year.

4. *Purpose, use, and security.* This section explains that the bond will be issued in three series to fund special obligations of the Authority, and that the obligations are pledged and secured by payments from the State of New York (future revenues).

scale: a summary of maturity dates, principal amounts, interest rates, and prices of a serial bond.

5. *Serial bond scale.* The *scale* is the summary of maturity dates, principal amounts, interest rates, and prices of the serial portion of the issue. In this sample, the serial bond is broken down into three groups, K, L, and M.

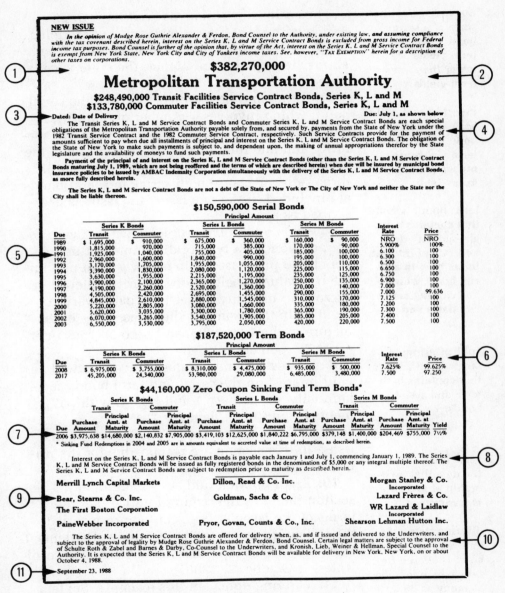

FIGURE 6–1 Official Statement Cover for a Municipal Bond
New Issue

normal scale: the scale of a serial bond when shorter-term yields are lower than longer-term yields.

inverted scale: the scale of a serial bond when shorter-term yields are higher than longer-term yields.

term bond: a bond that contains a single maturity date and rate of interest, in contrast to a serial bond, which has varying maturity dates and rates.

split offering: a single bond issue that contains both term and serial bonds.

settlement date: the date that ownership of securities is transferred.

offering date: the date a newly issued bond is offered for sale, which may be as many as 30 days prior to dated, or issue, date.

The scale is described as *"normal"* when bonds with shorter-term maturities offer yields lower than those on longer-term bonds. When shorter-term yields are higher, the scale is called *"inverted."*

6. *Term bond breakdown.* Unlike the serial bond, which involves a number of maturities over a period of years, term bonds have one maturity and one interest rate. In this example, the total issue includes two term bonds, issued in three series. Because both serial and term bonds are included in the one issue, the issue is described as a *split offering.*

7. *Zero coupon bond breakdown.* A zero coupon bond is a type of discounted issue in which the purchase value is lower than par but the par value is paid upon maturity. Interest is accrued to maturity rather than paid every six months. In the example, the three series each mature in the year 2006, and each accrues interest at 7½ percent.

8. *Interest payment dates.* Investors will be paid interest on the serial and term bonds semiannually, on January 1 and July 1, with payments beginning on January 1, 1989.

9. *Underwriting group.* The organizations listed in this section are responsible for the primary marketing of the issue.

10. *Legal opinion and settlement date.* This section includes the required notice that the terms of the issue are subject to approval that the indenture meets the terms of law. *Settlement date,* the earliest date investors can receive certificates, is October 4, 1988.

11. *Offering date.* In this example, September 23, 1988, is the commencement date of this issue. A distinction must be made between offering and dated, or issue, date. The *offering date* may be up to 30 days prior to dated date. The time delay may be necessary in order to complete printing the bond certificates and obtaining a final legal opinion.

JUDGING MUNICIPAL DEBT

Bond issuers are assigned a credit rating based on a study of financial strength, history of repayment, and comparisons of debt to taxing power and future revenue. However, the rating is only an estimate of relative safety. You may want to investigate a municipality on your own and ask a broker for details of the financial analysis that went into a rating.

A municipality's debt is divided into two types. *Floating debt* is the total of obligations due within five years or less, and *funded debt* is the total due with maturities beyond five years. These distinctions are industry terms for short-term and long-term debt. But they are not the same as the division between short-term notes and longer-term bonds. A bond issue may mature within the next five years, meaning that the floating debt will be greater than the total of outstanding notes.

floating debt: the total of a municipality's debts that will mature within five years or less.

funded debt: the total of a municipality's debts that will mature beyond five years.

These distinctions are important in your analysis of a municipality's safety. The ability to repay obligations rests on a comparison between two factors. First is the level and timing of interest payments and maturity of existing debts; second is the level of future tax or project revenue and the municipality's ability to increase revenues if necessary.

At the county and city level, your analysis can

be performed by comparing overall debt levels to the current market value of real estate. Current market value is used in this comparison because the difference between assessed and market value may be significant.

As a general rule, the ratio should not exceed 10 percent (meaning that total debt should not be greater than 10 percent of the current market value of taxable real property). Depending on how far apart the assessed value and the actual market value are, this rule may vary. If assessed value is higher in one county than in another, then tax revenues will be higher as well—even if the total market values in each county are similar.

The timing of interest and principal repayments should also be studied in light of the annual tax revenues the municipality will receive. Because taxing power is limited, an overly heavy tax burden in future years could point to the possibility of default.

As shown in Figure 6–2, the *overall debt to market value ratio* is computed by dividing overall debt (including all bonds and notes outstanding) by the actual market value of taxable properties in the municipality.

overall debt to market value: a ratio comparing a municipality's total debt obligations to actual current market value of real property in the area.

$$\frac{D}{M} = R$$

D = overall debt
M = actual market value
R = ratio

FIGURE 6–2 Formula for Overall Debt to Actual Market Value

Example: A county currently has $62.8 million in outstanding municipal debt. According to the latest available estimates, total taxable properties in the county have a current market value of $845 million. The ratio is:

$$\frac{\$62,800,000}{\$845,000,000} = 7.4\%$$

In this example, the ratio is less than 10 percent. By application of the general standard, the county is not overextended. However, what if it is currently offering a new bond issue for $40 million? That would increase overall debt to $102.8 million. Then the ratio would be:

$$\frac{\$102,800,000}{\$845,000,000} = 12.2\%$$

Under the 10 percent standard, the county may be overextended in its ratio of debt to current market value of properties.

Another ratio worth applying is *per capita debt*—the amount of municipal debt per person in the area—computed as shown in Figure 6–3. This ratio is useful in comparing debt levels between municipalities with varying populations, levels of service, levels of debt, and property

per capita debt: a ratio comparing a municipality's total debt to the population in the area.

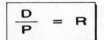

D = total debt
P = population
R = ratio

FIGURE 6–3 Formula for Per Capita Debt

values (both assessed and market value). When a county is growing rapidly, rapid construction of property adds to the tax base. Thus, the taxing power of the municipality expands as the population grows. The per capita debt ratio reveals whether a local debt level is growing, being maintained, or diminishing.

Example: A county has a population of 58,000 and total debts of $62.8 million. The per capita debt is:

$$\frac{\$62,800,000}{58,000} = \$1,082.76$$

Every resident of the county will have to pay this amount, which means that a family of four will pay, on average, $4,331.04 in future taxes just to retire outstanding municipal debt.

If the debt is increased to $102,800,000, but there is no change in the local population, the ratio will be:

$$\frac{\$102,800,000}{58,000} = \$1,772.41$$

This change represents a 64 percent increase in the per capita debt for the county.

The trend can move in another way, though. For example, the debt level might grow to $102,800,000, but the population might also grow to 100,000. Then the ratio would be:

$$\frac{\$102,800,000}{100,000} = \$1,028.00$$

In this example, the per capita debt declines by 5 percent, even though overall debt is increased.

The per capita analysis helps you to keep track of the changing status of a municipality's taxing power and debt management, even when the value of property and local population trends are on the move.

TAXATION OF MUNICIPAL BONDS

One of the most appealing features of muni bonds has always been their exemption from federal income taxes. In many cases, interest is also tax-free on the state and local levels. This special status was the result of a landmark case decided by the U.S. Supreme Court in 1895, *Pollock vs. Farmer's Loan and Trust Co.*, which established the principle that the federal government does not have the right to tax income derived from state and local debt.

This principle remained intact and unchallenged for 91 years until passage of the Tax Reform Act of 1986. That legislation modified the rules concerning taxation of municipal debt securities. Now these debts are defined and taxed in three groups:

1. *Public purpose bonds.* These are defined as bonds issued directly by a municipality (as opposed to an authority, district, or agency) and used to finance municipal projects. Public purpose bonds are still exempt from federal taxes.

2. *Private activity bonds.* This group includes debt securities issued by a municipality but used to finance private projects, such as sports stadiums or shopping malls. They are now taxed at the federal level, but continue to be exempt from state and local taxes.

3. *Nongovernmental purpose bonds.* This group includes bonds issued by a municipality whose proceeds are used for nonmunicipal purposes, such as the construction of new housing. Interest is tax-exempt at the federal level, but the annual amount is subject to limits. In addition, interest is treated as "preference income."

When interest from municipal bonds is treated as preference income, it is taxed through alternative minimum tax (AMT). If your overall income is largely derived from preference items, you could be subject to the AMT. The liability is computed in the normal way and then refigured under alternative rules; you will be liable for the higher of the two amounts. Preference items include interest from nongovernmental purpose bonds, depreciation, charitable contributions of appreciated securities, and income from the exercise of stock options.

The question of taxation applies only to interest received from a municipal investment; any capital gain (earned when the sale price of the bond is greater than the purchase price) is taxed under current capital gains rules. Furthermore, unlike bond interest, which receives special treatment, interest on municipal notes is usually fully taxed.

Municipal bonds may be attractive as tax-free investments not only on the federal level, but also for the exemption often allowed at the state and local level. If you live in the state of issue, most municipal bonds allow you to exempt interest from taxes. If the bond interest is also exempt from local taxes, investors will have a triple exemption.

Because municipal bond income is subject to exemption at one or more levels, a comparison between muni's and other investments should be made on an after-tax basis. For example, if you are considering buying a municipal bond that yields 6.5 percent interest, what is the after-tax equivalent for a taxable bond?

To compute the *equivalent taxable yield*, divide the municipal interest rate by your after-tax earnings rate (100 percent minus your effective tax rate). The formula is summarized in Figure 6–4.

equivalent taxable yield: a calculation that compares the after-tax yield of a taxable bond to the yield offered on a municipal bond.

Example: You want to compare a municipal bond yielding 6.5 percent to other investments. You will pay federal taxes this year at the rate of 33 percent. The equivalent taxable yield is:

$$\frac{.065}{1 - .33} = 9.7\%$$

To earn the same after-tax interest, a taxable investment must yield 9.7 percent per year.

The benefit of buying municipal bonds increases as your effective tax rate grows. This is especially important if you are subject to state and local taxes and the bond is exempt from tax at all levels.

Example: You are reviewing a municipal bond that yields 6.5 percent per year and comes with a triple exemption. Your tax rate at each level is:

Federal	33%
State	8
Local	3
Total	44%

$$\boxed{\frac{M}{1 - T} = Y}$$

M = municipal bond yield
T = tax rate
Y = equivalent yield

FIGURE 6–4 Formula for Equivalent Taxable Yield

In this case, the equivalent taxable yield is:

$$\frac{.065}{1 - .44} = 11.6\%$$

You would need to earn 11.6 percent per year just to match the yield from the tax-exempt bond. Thus, a taxable investment must exceed this level to produce a better yield.

Another aspect of the comparison of muni's and other bonds is the rating of each bond. For example, you might be able to locate a taxable debt security yielding above the equivalent taxable yield level, but would it be as safe as the municipal bond? If you can earn a greater after-tax rate, but the bond comes with a higher risk of default, the comparison is not valid.

Besides making comparisons on an after-tax basis, one standard you should apply is this: The safety rating of the taxable investment must be equal to or higher than the rating of the tax-exempt bond. Selecting a bond that fails this test may represent a much greater risk than you are willing to assume.

EVALUATING THE RISKS

The favorable tax status of muni bonds overcomes the tax risk associated with many forms of investment. At the same time, it exposes you to another form of risk—that the tax benefits will gain so much weight that you will forget to compare safety features. The financial strength of the issuer, represented by its ability to pay interest and principle, should be one of the most critical tests when comparing one bond to another.

Defaults are not widespread among municipal issues, and the few defaults that do occur are prominently featured in the press, perhaps because they are so unexpected and rare. However, default risk is real and should not be ignored.

You can select municipal bonds on the basis of the desired maturity to avoid the risk of illiquidity. Municipal bonds, like corporates, can have a discounted current market value, meaning that upon sale, you receive less than the face amount. But municipal bonds can be purchased with relatively short-term maturities—as little as a few months.

The usual minimum unit purchase is $5,000 for a single municipal bond, with some available in $1,000 units. For a modest portfolio, this poses the problem of diversification, but this can be minimized by including muni bonds as part of a broader diversification plan. Or you can invest through a tax-free municipal bond mutual fund or a unit investment trust (which invests in a fixed portfolio of tax-free bonds with varying maturities; unit investment trusts are discussed in detail in Chapter 10).

The most common types of municipal and other bonds are only part of the debt securities market. Other debt securities are available in various forms. These are described in the next chapter.

7

Other Debt Securities

Corporate, U.S. government, and municipal bonds are the three major, but not the only, categories of debt securities. You can also buy bonds issued internationally or by foreign issuers, and there is also a large market in short-term debt investments. Moreover, the traditional forms of bonds are available in discounted form.

In this chapter, we will explain international and foreign bonds; short-term debts broadly called the money market; and zero coupon bonds.

INTERNATIONAL AND FOREIGN BONDS

Two organizations help fund projects internationally. The International Bank for Reconstruction and Development (IBRD, also called the "World Bank") began operations in 1946. Its original intention was to finance reconstruction in European and Asian countries following World War II. Today, IBRD finances projects in developing countries around the world.

Institutions in the United States and other countries buy the bonds issued by IBRD, which then grants loans or guarantees loans for governments. Typical projects include industrial development, transportation systems, educational facilities, and power and utility plants. The United States controls approximately one-fourth of the voting power of IBRD.

The second organization is the Inter-American Development Bank (IADB). Founded in 1959, IADB finances projects of governments in the Western Hemisphere.

High inflation in foreign countries may lead to attractive interest rates on debt securities. However, the greater the rate of overseas inflation, the more volatile the investing and political situation may be. One way to overcome the individual risk of entering an uncertain market is to diversify into foreign bonds through global, international, or single-country mutual funds. While most of these funds concentrate on stock investments, many are balanced between growth and income and may include foreign debt securities.

The foreign market is complex and specialized, and the risks of investing will be an important consideration for anyone. You will need to work with a brokerage firm that has a foreign office and is familiar with the risks, rules of transaction, and transaction costs. The method of valuing a foreign security and identifying an issuer's financial stability may not be as consistent as in the United States, because regulations vary from one country to another.

THE MONEY MARKET

Most individual investors will shy away from the exotic world of foreign exchange and stick with domestic debt securities. Bonds, which may mature in 30 years or more, represent only one part of the total debt security market. Short-term debt investments (maturing in five years or less) may be suitable for your portfolio.

Short-term debts are generally referred to as "*paper*." We have already described some of these instruments in previous chapters. For example, a Treasury bill is the U.S. government's money market security. One variation is the *cash management bill*, a type of Treasury bill with maturity other than in 13, 26, or 52 weeks. This version of a T-bill is used to provide funds to the government in the short term, to be repaid from tax revenues to be received within a few days.

paper: any short-term debt security.

cash management bill: a Treasury bill issued irregularly and with a maturity other than 13, 26, or 52 weeks.

Municipal notes (tax, revenue, and bond anticipation notes) are also classified as money market instruments. Unlike municipal bonds, which may be held for many years, notes are distinguished by relatively short maturities. Other types of paper include:

1. *Banker's acceptance.* This is a letter of credit given by a financial institution to a manufacturer or supplier. The acceptance matures within six months and is used to provide funds to companies between delivery and payment dates. For example, a manufacturer delivers material to a user and uses a banker's acceptance to get immediate payment. Six months later, the user pays for the material and the manufacturer repays the banker's acceptance.

banker's acceptance: a letter of credit issued by a financial institution to finance transactions between the delivery date and the payment date.

call loan: a short-term loan made by a bank to a securities broker-dealer, which may be called with as little as one day's notice.

certificates of deposit (CD): debt instruments issued by financial institutions, which mature between seven days and five years, in denominations of $1 million or more.

commercial paper: an unsecured note issued by a corporation with a maturity from 3 to 270 days, used to provide operating funds when accounts receivable balances are outstanding.

federal funds: reserve balances in excess of requirements on deposit at a Federal Reserve bank.

repurchase agreement (repo): an agreement to sell securities and to repurchase them at a specified price and on a specified

2. *Call loans.* These are loans made by banks to securities broker-dealers. They are pledged by securities held by the brokerage firm. Either side in the transaction can cancel, or call, a call loan with one day's notice.

3. *Certificates of deposit.* These are short-term debts issued by financial institutions. Maturity ranges between seven days and five years, and denominations begin at $1 million. Interest is usually fixed, although some variations of CDs include periodically adjusted interest rates. This CD is not the same as the smaller certificates issued for a few hundred dollars, to the public. While its name is the same, the smaller CD is a variation of a time deposit account.

4. *Commercial paper.* Commercial paper is unsecured short-term notes issued by corporations to finance accounts receivables that are outstanding. Maturity ranges between 3 and 270 days. For example, a corporation has a large balance of accounts receivable due from customers. It issues commercial paper to provide working capital until the receivables have been paid. Upon receipt, the commercial paper investors are repaid.

5. *Federal funds.* These are excess reserves of commercial banks, on deposit in Federal Reserve banks, which may be loaned to other member banks short-term. Interest is charged at the federal funds rate.

6. *Repurchase agreement (repo).* A repo is an agreement to sell securities and then to buy them back at a specified price and on a specified date in the near future, often in 24 hours. The repo is used to borrow money that is invested in securities.

7. *Reverse repurchase agreement.* This is a variation of the repo, in which one side agrees to buy securities and then resell them at a specified price and date, plus interest. The reverse repo may be used to deliver securities that have been sold short.

Most money market transactions occur between financial institutions and corporations and involve large amounts of money. You can invest in a diversified portfolio of short-term debt instruments by purchasing shares in a money market mutual fund. Similar programs, called money market accounts, can be opened at many banks, savings and loan associations, or credit unions.

future date (often the next day). The repo is used to borrow money invested in securities.

reverse repurchase agreement: an agreement to buy securities and to resell them at a specified price and on a specified future date, with interest. The reverse repo is used to deliver securities that have been sold short.

DISCOUNTED BOND INVESTING

The money market is an alternative to the relatively long-term requirements of bond investing. With short-term debt instruments, your funds can be kept fairly liquid. In a money market fund, for example, you enjoy extremely high liquidity, since you can withdraw funds by simply writing a check against your account's balance.

Another way to purchase debt instruments and avoid long-term commitment of funds is through *zero coupon bonds*. These are bonds issued at a deep discount, which attain par value at maturity. You may select zero coupon bonds with either relatively short- or longer-term maturities—all depending on the time period you want to invest. This makes zero coupons ideal for building up funds with a specific future deadline in mind (such as a child's college education, retirement, or a down payment for the purchase of a home).

zero coupon bond: a bond issued at discount, with interest accreted during the period until maturity and with par value paid at maturity date.

accreted interest: the method of crediting interest earned on a zero coupon bond. Rather than paying interest twice per year, the bond increases its current market value by a level representing the compound yield.

A term bond is typically purchased at or near par, and interest is paid twice per year. With a *zero coupon bond*, the purchase price may be quite small—as little as $100 or $200. Instead of receiving interest twice per year, the current value of the bond increases over the holding period. Thus, interest is not paid, but is accrued, or "*accreted.*"

The original issue discount feature is not a new idea, although the popularity and availability of zero coupon bonds has grown during recent years. Series EE bonds are the U.S. government's version of original discount issue; now Treasury bills are also issued in discount form.

Example: A zero coupon bond matures in five years and offers a yield of 8 percent. The purchase price is $675.56. Interest is accreted every six months, so during the five years, the bond's value will grow 10 times, at the compound rate of 4 percent (8 percent divided by two semiannual periods).

This schedule can be proven by multiplying each period's beginning value by 1.04, as shown in Table 7–A.

The formula for interest accretion is shown in Figure 7–1. The purchase price is multiplied by 1 plus the semiannual rate for the number of periods between purchase and maturity. In our example, the formula is applied at the annual rate of 8 percent (4 percent every six months). The purchase price was $675.56, so interest during the first period is:

$$675.56 \times (1 + .04) - 675.56 = 27.02$$

TABLE 7–A   Schedule of Accreted Interest on an 8-Percent Zero Coupon Bond

Month	Value	Interest
	$ 675.56	$27.02
6	702.58	28.11
12	730.69	29.22
18	759.91	30.40
24	790.31	31.61
30	821.92	32.88
36	854.80	34.19
42	888.99	35.56
48	924.55	36.98
54	961.53	38.47
60	1,000.00	$324.44

When the first period's accreted interest is added to the previous value, the next period's value is the result:

$$
\begin{array}{r}
27.02 \\
+\ 675.56 \\
\hline
702.58
\end{array}
$$

The same steps are repeated for each period to maturity.

$$P \times (1 + r)^n - P = A$$

P = purchase price
r = semiannual rate
n = number of periods
A = accreted interest

FIGURE 7–1   Formula for Interest Accretion

Accreted interest is a *compound* rate of interest. Thus, buying zero coupon bonds gives you the benefit of compounding, whereas a term bond does not. For example, you may invest in a term bond paying 8 percent interest, but unless you are able to reinvest interest at 8 percent, you will not gain the benefits of compounding.

In comparison to a zero coupon bond, a term bond maturing in five years and paying 8 percent interest will show a different compounding history. Assuming the bond is bought at par, the basis will be $1,000, and you will receive $40 in each of the 10 semiannual periods. After five years, you will be paid the $1,000 par value.

With a term bond, total interest adds up to $400, compared to $324.44 with the zero coupon bond. But with the zero coupon choice, your original investment was only $675.56, compared with $1,000 in the term bond. Thus, the rate of return is greater. You could purchase three zero coupon bonds with slightly more than $2,000, but for the same money, you could afford only two term bonds at par. At the same interest rate, total income from each would be:

Zero coupon bond:
$$3 \times 324.44 = 973.32$$
Term bond:
$$2 \times 400.00 = \underline{800.00}$$
Difference: 173.32

You can prove the compounding effects in a zero coupon bond by multiplying the semiannual rate by the purchase price for each of the periods until maturity. Based on a purchase price of $675.56, a five-year maturity, and 8 percent interest per year, what is the compounded effect?

The first period's interest is compounded at

the semiannual rate nine times (because there are nine semiannual periods remaining until maturity). The second period's interest is compounded for eight periods, and the number of periods thereafter is reduced every six months. The computation begins with a calculation of 4 percent of the purchase price:

$$675.56 \times .04 = 27.02$$

Table 7–B shows exactly how the computation is done. A few cents are lost to rounding, but it still proves that a zero coupon bond's interest, unlike a term bond's, is compounded.

The calculation involves several steps, but fortunately there is an easier way to arrive at the same result. We can refer to a compound interest table for the future worth of one dollar per period, computed semiannually. This table shows the compounded value at 8 percent for any num-

TABLE 7–B   Schedule of Compounding for a Five-Year, 8-Percent Zero Coupon Bond

Month	Interest	Periods	Multiplier	Compound Value
6	27.02	9	$(1.04)^9$	38.46
12	27.02	8	$(1.04)^8$	36.98
18	27.02	7	$(1.04)^7$	35.56
24	27.02	6	$(1.04)^6$	34.19
30	27.02	5	$(1.04)^5$	32.87
36	27.02	4	$(1.04)^4$	31.61
42	27.02	3	$(1.04)^3$	30.39
48	27.02	2	$(1.04)^2$	29.22
54	27.02	1	$(1.04)^1$	28.10
60	27.02	0	$(1.04)^0$	27.02
				324.40

ber of years. The factor on that table for five
years is 12.006107. Multiply this by 4 percent
interest based on the purchase price:

$$12.006107 \times 27.02 = 324.41$$

To match a zero coupon bond's yield with a
term bond's, you need to reinvest each interest
payment at the same rate paid on the bond.
Thus, if you invest $1,000 and receive $40.00
every six months, you calculate the compound
yield using the same table:

$$12.006107 \times 40.00 = 480.24$$

These calculations prove a stated interest rate
on a zero coupon bond. However, you may also
need to calculate the yield only on the basis of
the current purchase price. In that case, you will
need to figure out the present value, which is
the opposite of future value.

COMPUTING ZERO COUPON YIELD

Future value tells you the compounded value of
interest received over a number of semiannual
periods. Present value is the value at the beginning of a term, when the final value is known. In
our zero coupon bond example, we know that
the future (maturity) value is $1,000. And we
need to determine what interest rate is represented by today's purchase price of $675.56.

In the "Present Value of One Dollar Compound Interest" table, the five-year factor
for semiannual compounding at 8 percent is
0.675564. If we multiply this by the maturity

value of the bond, we will arrive at today's price:

$$0.675564 \times 1,000 = 675.56$$

A bond quotation gives you only the maturity date and the closing price, however. For example, in 1990, a zero coupon bond of the XYZ Company is listed in this manner:

$$\text{ABC Corp. zr95 } \frac{\text{close}}{66}$$

This tells you that the bond matures in five years (from 1990 to 1995) and that today's price is 66, or $660.00. But what is the yield?

You can estimate the answer by using the "Present Value of One Dollar Semiannual Interest" table. A sampling reveals the following five-year factors:

year	7%	7½%	8%	8½%
5	0.708919	0.692020	0.675564	0.659537

To calculate the interest rate, study the factors for 8 and for 8½ percent. We know that the maturity value of the bond is $1,000, so the yield must fall somewhere between these percentages:

8%:
$$0.675564 \times \$1,000 = 675.56$$

8½%:
$$0.659537 \times \$1,000 = 659.54$$

We can estimate the factor for 8¼ percent by calculating the average of the two known factors:

$$\frac{0.675564 + 0.659537}{2} = 0.667551$$

We now can estimate that the yield on the zero coupon bond lies somewhere between 8¼ percent and 8½ percent:

$8^1/_4\%$ factor = 0.667551, or $667.55
current price = $660.00
$8^1/_2\%$ factor = 0.659537, or $659.54

Yield, of course, is only one element in the selection factor. Zero coupon bonds are issued by the U.S. government, by corporations, and by municipalities. You may even purchase a zero coupon version of money market debt, called the zero CD. The decision of which ones to include in your portfolio should be based on the safety you need and want, compared with the available yields.

STRIPS: Separate Trading of Registered Interest and Principal of Securities.

The more popular zero coupon bonds on U.S. government securities include *STRIPS*, or Separate Trading of Registered Interest and Principal of Securities, which are zero coupons of U.S. government securities. You may also invest in *CATS*, or Certificate of Accrual in Treasury Securities, or in *TIGRs*, Treasury Investment Growth Receipts.

CATS: Certificate of Accrual on Treasury Securities.

TIGRs: Treasury Investment Growth Receipts.

EVALUATING THE RISKS

Zero coupon bonds, like most bonds, offer a fixed rate of interest. This may be a market advantage if future rates fall, or it may be a disadvantage if today's rates turn out to be lower than the average. The shorter the term to maturity of a zero coupon bond, the lower your interest-rate risk.

The greatest advantage of zero coupon bonds is that the interest is compounded. Except through a bond mutual fund, the same advantage is not possible with a term bond, for which interest is paid out every six months. Thus, with term bonds your portfolio's value does not benefit from compound interest, unless you are able to reinvest at the same or better rate. Or, if current rates are lower than the rates on a term bond, the effect of compounding will be less beneficial than with a comparable zero coupon bond.

The zero coupon bond produces not only a predictable yield, but a known future maturity value and date. You may diversify your portfolio with a range of maturities based on your personal investing goals. If you want your bonds to mature within five to ten years, you will be able to find discounted bonds that will meet that goal. And if your goal is longer-term, the cost of the bond—as well as the yield—will be much lower.

Because the purchase price of a zero coupon bond is well below par value, you will be able to afford more bonds and, potentially, greater diversification with the same money. For example, with $10,000, you may purchase a mixture of:

1. 10 term bonds, for $1,000 each
2. 20 zero coupon bonds, for an average cost of $500 each
3. 40 zero coupon bonds, for an average cost of $250 each

The major risks associated with zero coupon bonds relate to safety and taxation. The higher-yielding zero coupon bond is likely to be as risky as a higher-yielding term bond. The credit rating of the issuer is the key to identifying an appropriate risk level.

phantom interest:
interest that is taxable each year but not received in cash.

Zero coupon bond interest is taxed each year, even though you do not receive money. This is called *phantom interest*. The problem of phantom interest may be significant to an investor with a great deal of money invested in zero coupons, but to those with a relatively small amount of capital invested, it is not a great concern. For example, if you invest cash in a passbook savings account, you are taxed on interest even if you do not withdraw funds to pay your taxes. The result in this situation is the same as that with zero coupon bonds: The tax must be paid, even if the investment's compounding value is left intact.

An exception to the phantom interest rule is the Series EE bond. You have the choice of paying taxes each year or deferring the liability until maturity. Most investors choose the latter. Even at maturity, you can continue the deferral by exchanging EE bonds for HH bonds.

If a bond can be exchanged for another bond (or for shares of stock), it is called a convertible bond. Convertibles are explained in the next chapter.

8

Convertible Bonds

One type of corporate bond can be redeemed either by holding it until maturity or by exchanging it for the company's common stock. This decision is made not by the issuer, but by the investor.

The *convertible bond* is most often a junior subordinated debenture. This means your investment has a greater degree of risk than other corporate bonds, for two reasons:

1. The convertible bond is not secured. You will recall that debentures are backed by the corporation's promise alone.

2. It is a subordinated debt. Thus, in the event of liquidation, other bondholders will be repaid before holders of subordinated debts.

With these points in mind, you should base your selection of a convertible bond on the issuer's financial strength. That should be a critical point in your evaluation process.

convertible bond: a corporate bond, usually a junior subordinated debenture, that can be exchanged for shares of the issuer's common stock.

conversion privilege: the bondholder's right to exchange the debt position of a bond for an equity position in the issuer's common stock.

Debentures, because they are unsecured, usually offer a greater yield than do collateralized bonds from the same issuer. However, the *conversion privilege* is a distinct advantage to you, and because of that advantage, the yield on convertible debentures will be lower than on comparable bonds from the same issuer and with the same maturity date.

This point could confuse an investor who is aware of the relationship between yield and risk. As a general rule, the greater the yield, the greater the risk. So a convertible bond analyzed just on that basis could appear to be a lower risk than another bond. In fact, though, the yield doesn't tell the whole story. The potential for growth in the value of common stock must also be brought into the question.

Corporations issue convertible debentures for a number of reasons. For example, they might believe that conversion is preferable to a long schedule of interest payments, especially if the stock's future value will be much greater than it is at the time the bond is issued. The corporation may also issue a convertible to hold down the cost of borrowing money. The issuer may offer a relatively low interest rate, knowing that investors will be attracted to the conversion feature.

A company may need to raise capital, but may not want to issue more shares of stock. To do so would dilute earnings for existing shareholders and, in the opinion of the directors, would make it impossible to maintain the earnings per share established in the past. A solution is to issue convertible debentures, paying interest below the current market rates.

This strategy assumes that, in the event the stock's value rises, so that the bonds are converted, the increase in market value will offset

the transfer from debt to equity. At the same
time, it will reduce the company's requirement
to continue paying interest on the bonds, as conversion will retire the debt.

A bond may be both convertible and callable.
In that instance, the call feature may apply for a
limited period of time, so the corporation will
have the option of making a call or letting it
pass. The call might be exercised as a way to
force conversion if the issuer prefers that investors assume equity positions over debt positions.
Or the issuer might simply want to reserve the
right to retire a debt before maturity, even when
investors have a conversion privilege.

FEATURES OF CONVERTIBLE SECURITIES

If the company's stock value does rise, the market value of the convertible bond will follow suit
—although it will not grow in value dollar for
dollar. Eventually, a rising stock value will mean
that owning stock is more profitable than owning the bond, making conversion the obvious
choice. The converted bond will be retired not
by paying interest twice per year all the way to
maturity, but by issuing stock in replacement.

If the stock falls in value, the convertible bond
will also fall, but it will fall at a slower rate.
There is a limit to how far the bond's value will
decline, regardless of losses in the stock. That is
because the bond has value as a debt security,
which is called _investment value_. That value is
determined on the basis of time to maturity and
the interest rate, compared with other market
rates (meaning that the bond may sell at a premium or discount, reflecting demand as well as
the value of the interest rate the bond pays).

**investment
value: an estimate
set by a bond ana-
lyst of what a con-
vertible bond's
lowest likely mar-
ket value would be
without the conver-
sion privilege, as-
suming that market
interest rates re-
main stable.**

Following is a summary of a convertible bond's features:

1. It will change in market value not only because of changes in market interest rates and investor demand, but also because of market value changes in the issuer's stock. A convertible is a hybrid investment. It contains features of both equity and debt securities.

2. Convertible bondholders receive interest twice per year, just as nonconvertible bondholders do. The contractual terms of the bond do not change just because it is convertible.

3. Convertible bond values will change in the same direction as the issuer's stock will. But there is a limit to how far values will fall, since the bond has value as a debt security. This is called investment value. It is determined by analysts and represents the lowest likely value the bond could hold if it did not have a conversion feature. Investment value also is based on the assumption that prevailing market interest rates will not change. (Investment value is not fixed. As interest rates move, the convertible bond's investment value is reassessed accordingly.)

CONVERSION PRICE AND RATIO

conversion price: the price per share at which a bond may be converted to common stock, specified in the indenture or computed by dividing the bond's par value by the conversion ratio.

When a convertible bond is issued, the indenture includes either a *conversion price* or a *conversion ratio*. The conversion price is the price per share you will receive if and when the bond is converted.

Example: A convertible bond's indenture specifies that the conversion price is $50. If the stock's value rises above $50 per share while you own the bond, conversion will become likely because the stock's value will be greater than the par value of the bond.

An exception to this rule comes up when the current market value of the bond is at such a premium that the bond has greater value than the stock.

Example: The conversion price is $50, and the stock's current market value is $52 per share, meaning that you could convert and acquire stock for $2 per share below current market value. Since the par value of the bond is $1,000, you could pick up 20 shares at the conversion price:

$$\$50 \times 20 \text{ shares} = \$1,000$$

The market value of those 20 shares is $52 per share:

$$\$52 \times 20 \text{ shares} = \$1,040$$

However, if the bond has a current value of 106, it would not make sense to convert:

Bond's market value, $106 =	$1,060
Stock's market value, $52 =	1,040
Difference	$ 20

The bond's market value is greater than the stock's, even though the market value of the stock is above the conversion price.

The indenture may specify a conversion ratio rather than a price per share. This tells you how many shares you will receive upon conversion.

Example: A bond's indenture includes a conversion privilege stating that you have the right to exchange the bond for 20 shares of common stock. In fact, this is the same conversion privi-

conversion ratio: the number of shares to be received upon conversion, specified in the indenture or computed by dividing the bond's par value by the conversion price.

lege as the one granted at $50 per share. Computed either way, the result equals the par value of the bond.

> **Ratio:**
> 20 shares @ $50 = $1,000
> **Price:**
> $50 @ 20 shares = $1,000

You can compute the conversion price if you know the conversion ratio. The formula is shown in Figure 8–1.

Example: The bond indenture states that the conversion ratio is 20 (meaning you can exchange the bond for 20 shares of common stock). The conversion price is $50 per share:

$$\frac{\$1,000}{20} = \$50$$

You can also compute the conversion ratio, as long as you know the conversion price, simply by reversing the formula, as shown in Figure 8–2.

Example: The bond indenture states that the conversion price is $50 (meaning that you can exchange the bond for shares at the price of $50 per share). The conversion ratio is 20 (shares):

$$\frac{\$1,000}{\$50} = 20$$

$$\boxed{\frac{B}{R} = C}$$

B = par value of bond
R = conversion ratio
C = conversion price

FIGURE 8–1 Formula for Conversion Price

$$\frac{B}{C} = R$$

B = par value of bond
C = conversion price
R = conversion ratio

FIGURE 8–2   Formula for Conversion Ratio

You will need to know the conversion level (whether stated as a price for share, as a ratio, or as a number of shares) in order to figure out the conversion value during the time you own the bond.

Conversion price and ratio will be adjusted for dividends declared and paid as well as for any stock splits. In the case of a split, the stock's value does not change. A split is nothing more than an adjustment in the number of shares outstanding and in the value of those shares.

Example: A company's stock is currently valued at $50 per share. A 2 for 1 split is declared. From that point forward, investors own twice as much stock with half as much value per share. Thus, an investor who previously owned 100 shares would own 200 shares after the split, and the owner of a convertible bond having a conversion price of $50 would experience an adjustment to $25.

As the result of a split, the conversion ratio is doubled—from 20 to 40 shares. This does not change the value, it only adjusts the numbers. The change is made to both the conversion price and ratio (these are simply different expressions of the same value):

Before the split:
20 shares @ $50 = $1,000

After the split:
40 shares @ $25 = $1,000

CONVERSION VALUE AND PREMIUM

conversion value:
the current market
value of common
stock based on the
conversion ratio of
a bond. It is com-
puted by multiply-
ing the conversion
ratio by the stock's
current value per
share.

Once you know the conversion ratio, you can
identify the *conversion value* of the stock. This
is nothing more than the current market value
based on the stock's price and the number of
shares you would receive.

Example: The conversion ratio is 20, and par
value of the bond is $1,000. You track the
stock's market value over a period of weeks and
note the following changes:

Week	Stock's Value
1	$47
2	50
3	52

The conversion value is computed by multiplying the conversion ratio by the current market
value of the stock (see Figure 8–3):

**conversion pre-
mium:** the differ-
ence between a
bond's market
value and its con-
version value,
divided by con-
version value. It
is expressed as a
percentage repre-
senting an estimate
of investors' per-
ceptions about the
convertible bond's
current value.

Week 1:
20 × $47 = $940
Week 2:
20 × $50 = $1,000
Week 3:
20 × $52 = $1,040

The value of having the conversion privilege
depends not on the bond's par value, but on the
comparison of market values between the bond
and the stock. The *conversion premium* is a calculation of this value. It is a percentage that represents an estimate of investors' perception

$$\boxed{R \times S = V}$$

R = conversion ratio
S = market value of stock
V = conversion value

FIGURE 8–3 Formula for Conversion Value

about the convertible bond's current value. Because the bond's market value is adjusted on the basis of demand, it reflects an opinion about safety, yield, and time to maturity—the points that determine supply and demand. With a convertible bond, a new element of value enters and must be calculated. The conversion premium is the difference between the conversion value and the market value of a bond.

Example: Conversion value is $940, based on a ratio of 20 (shares) and the stock's current market value of $47 per share (20 × $47 = $940). The bond is currently valued at 103 ($1,030). The conversion premium is computed in the following steps (see Figure 8–4 for the formula):

1. Subtract conversion value from the current market value of the bond:

$$\$1,030 - \$940 = \$90$$

2. Divide the answer in step 1 by the conversion value:

$$\frac{\$90}{\$940} = .0957$$

3. Find the percentage equivalent of the decimal answer by moving the decimal point two places to the right:

$$.0957 = 9.57\%$$

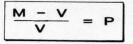

$$\frac{M - V}{V} = P$$

M = market value of bond
V = conversion value
P = conversion premium

FIGURE 8–4   Formula for Conversion Premium

The market value of this bond has a conversion premium of 9.57 percent above the conversion value, based on the current value of the issuer's stock.

PREMIUM OVER INVESTMENT VALUE

premium over investment value: the percentage difference between market value and investment value, divided by investment value; the current value of the conversion privilege.

Premium over investment value, as illustrated in Figure 8–5, is the percentage difference between market value and investment value, divided by investment value. Investment value, you recall, is an estimate of the lowest likely value the bond could have, assuming that the conversion feature is absent and that current interest rates will not change in the future.

Example: Your convertible bond's current market price is 100 ($1,000). In the analyst's

$$\frac{M - I}{I} = O$$

M = market value of bond
I = investment value
O = premium over
investment value

FIGURE 8–5   Formula for Premium over Investment Value

opinion, that bond's investment value is 82. The calculation for premium over investment value represents the value of your conversion privilege. It is computed by first subtracting investment value from the bond's current market value and then dividing that answer by investment value:

$$\frac{100 - 82}{82} = 22.0\%$$

In other words, if the analyst's estimate of investment value is accurate, then the conversion privilege is worth 22 percent more than that value.

The many computations possible for convertible bonds can be studied together on a single schedule. Table 8–A shows how the various tests come out based on a bond at par, an increase in the stock's value, and a decrease in the stock's value. We have included the current yield on the bond (annual interest receipts di-

TABLE 8–A   Convertible Bond Analysis

	Bond at Par	Stock Rises	Stock Falls
Market price of bond	$1,000	$1,200	$820
Current yield	10.00%	8.33%	12.20%
Conversion ratio	20	20	20
Conversion price	$50	$50	$50
Market price of stock	$35	$43	$28
Conversion value	$700	$860	$560
Conversion premium	42.9%	39.5%	46.4%
Investment value	$820	$820	$820
Premium over investment value	22.0%	46.3%	0.0%

vided by current market value of the bond), so that the analysis can be performed comprehensively. In this example, the 10 percent nominal rate, based on a par value of $1,000, is $100 per year in interest.

These calculations can be verified by applying the formulas that affect results for each line on the table. For example, testing the results on the basis of values shown in the middle column (stock rises):

Current yield:
$$\frac{\$100}{\$1,200} = 8.33\%$$
Conversion ratio:
$$\frac{\$1,000}{\$50} = 20$$
Conversion price:
$$\frac{\$1,000}{20} = \$50$$
Conversion value:
$$20 \times \$43 = \$860$$
Conversion premium:
$$\frac{\$1,200 - \$860}{\$860} = 39.5\%$$
Premium over investment value:
$$\frac{\$1,200 - \$820}{\$820} = 46.3\%$$

FINDING PARITY

parity: the market price of a convertible bond at which the bond and the common stock of the issuer are identical in market value.

In addition to determining the value of the conversion privilege, you will also need to know at what point the bond and common stock are of equal value, considering that the bond's value is likely to change each time the stock's value moves up or down. This is called *parity*. Parity is an easy way to determine whether or not conversion makes sense on the basis of current market value of stock.

Example: Your bond has a par value of $1,000 and is convertible at the price of $50 per share. The current market price of stock is $64 per share. Parity is calculated by dividing the par value by the conversion price and then comparing that to the unknown parity level divided by the stock's current market value:

$$\frac{\$1,000}{\$50} = \frac{x}{\$64}$$

The parity value of the bond is the unknown, 'x' in this equation. The left side can be reduced so that the equation reads:

$$20 \times \frac{x}{\$64}$$

Next, the unknown 'x' is isolated by moving the stock's market value to the right side. Multiply both sides of the equation by $64:

$$20 \times \$64 = x$$

The answer:

$$\$1,280 = x$$

The bond's market value must be 128 ($1,280) to achieve parity. The formula is summarized in Figure 8–6.

Once you have computed parity, compare the answer to the bond's current market value. If the bond is below the level of 128, you will profit by converting the bond. However, if the bond has a market price above that level, then it will make sense to not exercise the conversion privilege.

Example: Your bond has a current market price of 128, that is, exactly at parity with the stock. If you sell the bond today, you will re-

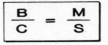

B = par value of bond
C = conversion price
M = market value of bond
S = market value of stock

FIGURE 8–6 Formula for Parity

ceive $1,280. If you convert to common stock with a market value of $64 per share, you will receive 20 shares:

$$20 \times \$64 = \$1,280$$

Example: Your bond has a current market price of 123, and the stock's market value is $64 per share. By converting to 20 shares of common stock, you will gain more value than you will by keeping the bond or by selling it:

Conversion value:
20 × $64 = $1,280
Bond market value: $1,230
Difference: $ 50

Parity and conversion value produce the same answer. You will recall that the conversion ratio multiplied by the current market value of stock produces conversion value. Parity, however, can help to identify a future breakeven point between the convertible bond and the stock. The calculation can be turned around to identify a parity stock price based on today's market value of a bond.

Example: Your bond has a current market value of 113, and the conversion ratio is 20. At what price will the common stock be at parity with the bond?

To calculate, divide the bond's current market value by the conversion ratio:

$$\frac{\$1,130}{20} = 56.5$$

When the stock's market value is at $56.50 per share, it is at parity with the bond, which has a current market value of 113.

OTHER FORMS OF CONVERTIBLE SECURITIES

Corporations sometimes sweeten a bond offering by giving investors the right to buy shares of common stock whether or not they convert the bond. This right is called a warrant or a subscription warrant, and when bonds are marketed in this manner, they are called *bonds with warrants attached*. The offering usually is made only with the issue of a senior debt security.

bonds with warrants attached: corporate bonds, usually senior debts, with which investors gain the right, through subscription warrants, to purchase a specified number of shares of the issuer's common stock.

The warrant itself has no intrinsic value, since it is neither a tangible debt obligation nor a share of ownership and gains tangible value only if exercised. But because the stock's value may rise or fall after bonds with warrants attached have been issued, the market value of the warrants changes as well—just as options change based on changes in the value of underlying stock.

Each warrant grants you the right to buy a specified number of shares at a specified price. The warrant will be in effect for only a certain period of time, which is spelled out in the bond's indenture. The warrant period does not always begin at issue date, but may go into effect at some later point. The period usually lasts 10 years or less.

A warrant can be exercised by the bondholder at any time after the period begins and before it expires. Warrants can also be sold separately from the bond or included with the bond at the time of sale. If the market value of the underlying stock is higher than the warrant price, then the market value of the bond with warrants attached will be correspondingly higher as well. And even if the stock's price is lower than the warrant level, these rights will have some value. Thus, when you sell the bond with the warrants, a premium will be added to the bond's current debt security value.

convertible preferred stock: a class of preferred corporate stock that can be exchanged for a specified value in common stock.

Another form of convertible security is an equity investment to begin with. *Convertible preferred stock* can be exchanged for a specified number of shares of common stock. Preferred stock has features that should be compared with those of both bonds and common stock. First, it has a priority of claim over the issuer's common stock, both for dividend payments and for liquidation. However, it is junior to all forms of debt securities.

The owner of convertible preferred shares may want to exchange them for common stock for a number of reasons. For example, the common stock might be paying a higher dividend yield, or the investor might believe the common stock has better potential for price appreciation.

The analysis of securities with conversion privileges is more complex than when no conversion rights are offered. The combined evaluation of yield, time to maturity, form of collateral if any, and financial strength of the issuer— along with the value of the conversion privilege —determines a convertible security's value.

The next chapter explains where you can find

information about the bond market. Included are the rating and research services, safety rankings, bond quotations and news in financial publications, and both technical and fundamental analysis as it applies to the debt securities market.

9

Information Sources

Bond investors rely on three primary sources
for market information. These are the published
ratings (showing relative safety of each bond); financial newspapers (for news about issuers and
the market as well as quotations for each classification of bond); and additional published
sources that compare prices and provide market
analysis. We will explain these sources in this
chapter. In addition, we will define some of the
popular analytical methods and rules of thumb
used in the industry.

You may depend on a broker's advice or work
with a financial planner or consultant in deciding to invest in bonds. As long as your adviser is
an expert in the bond market and uses current
published information to back up his or her rec-
ommendations, he or she will save you a lot of
time and trouble. However, you should ensure
that this is the case before taking someone else's
advice. If a broker does not use current informa-

tion sources to back up a recommendation, then you will have no sound basis for the investment decision. Your actions in the bond market, as in any investment market, will be as valuable as the information on which those actions are based—whether developed on your own or based on a recommendation.

BOND RATING SERVICES

A bond's rating tells you how safe it is as an investment. The rating is actually a commentary on the issuer's financial strength and its ability to repay principal and to continue making timely interest payments.

Remember that there is a clear relationship between yield and risk. The higher-yielding bonds come with a greater risk, and the safer, more secure bonds offer a correspondingly lower yield. You will be able to choose the bond best for you by identifying the risk level you are willing to assume.

The rating assigned to a company and the bonds it issues reflects the risk to you as an investor. Each rating service examines the financial security of the issuer, its history of repayment, and the collateral, if any, of the bond. The services then assign a rating to each bond and publish their findings. This is a judgment as to the issuer's credit quality.

The rating assigned by one of the independent bond rating services is not a recommendation to buy or to not buy. The services do not audit the company being evaluated, but depend largely on information supplied by the issuer. The rating is no more than an estimation of credit risk, which should be one of the bases for making your decision—and not the sole means for arriving at a conclusion about the safety or appropriateness of bond investing. Remember, too, that during the time the bond is outstanding, a rating may change on the basis of new information about the issuer.

Example: A company has issued a bond in order to introduce a new product. Two years later, the product is withdrawn because the market did not respond as the company had hoped. As a consequence, the profit prospects for the company are lower. The rating services respond by lowering their ratings for the bond. The market value of that bond will probably decline as a result, and investors seeking a lower degree of risk will probably sell their holdings on the open market. So rating status may affect the market value of a bond at any time between issue and maturity.

The three major rating services are:

Fitch Investors Service
5 Hanover Square
New York NY 10004

Moody's Investors Service
99 Church Street
New York NY 10007

Standard & Poor's Corporation (S&P)
26 Broadway
New York NY 10004

The *safety ratings* each service applies to corporate bonds are summarized in Figure 9–1. Except for short-term municipal obligations, these ratings are usually applied to municipal bond issues as well.

Safety is defined in four major groups: high-

safety ratings: a rating of bonds by one of three organizations: Fitch Investors Service, Moody's Investors Service, and Standard & Poor's Corporation.

DESCRIPTION	FITCH	MOODY'S	S & P
highest quality	AAA AA A	Aaa Aa A	AAA AA A
medium quality	BBB BB B	Baa Ba B	BBB BB B
poor quality	CCC CC C	Caa Ca C	CCC CC C
lowest quality	DDD DD D		D

FIGURE 9–1 Safety Ratings for Corporate Bonds by Rating Service and Quality Category

investment grade (bank quality): a bond with a rating between AAA (Aaa) and BBB (Baa). Ratings below this range are speculative grades.

est, medium, poor, and lowest quality. Bonds rated AAA (Aaa), AA, A, or BBB (Baa) are referred to as "*investment grade*" (or *bank quality*). There is very little risk of default with these bonds, and investors seeking safety for their capital will want to purchase bonds only within that range. Below the investment grade range, bonds are increasingly speculative.

THE MEANING OF RATING SYMBOLS

The corporate and municipal bond ratings used by each of the three organizations have similar definitions. These are[1]:

[1]These ratings are composites from the following sources: *Fitch Investors Service, Inc. Rating Register; S&P's Municipal Finance Criteria; Moody's Industrial Manual*

AAA (Aaa)—highest quality. The issuer has exceptional ability to repay.

AA (Aa)—high quality. The issuer has very strong ability to repay.

A—good quality. The issuer has strong ability to repay.

BBB (Baa)—satisfactory quality. The issuer has adequate ability to repay.

BB (Ba)—below investment grade, considered as speculative; the issuer's ability to repay is not strong.

B—highly speculative; the issuer's ability to repay is poor.

CCC (Caa)—the bond is vulnerable to default.

CC (Ca)—the bond is minimally protected; default seems probable.

C—the bond is in default or default is imminent.

DDD, DD, and D—in default; to be purchased for liquidation value only.

The actual definitions used by each rating service may vary slightly, but the purpose is clear: A change from one rating level to another indicates a slightly higher or lower opinion concerning the safety of that bond as an investment.

Each service has additional rating codes or symbols to further explain its ratings. For example, Fitch uses these signals:

(+) or (−)—these symbols appear after the rating to indicate finer distinctions of positive or negative opinion.

NR—a rating was not requested or was not completed in time for publication.

SUSPENDED—the rating is suspended due to inadequate information.

WITHDRAWN—the rating is withdrawn because the issuer did not supply timely information.

CONDITIONAL—the rating is conditional, based on assumptions about timely completion of a project being financed by the bond issue.

FITCH ALERT—the issue is under review, and a change in the rating is possible. An ALERT may be UP (positive implication); DOWN (negative implication); or EVOLVING (the direction of the change in rating is not certain).

Fitch also rates money market instruments:

Commercial paper ratings

Fitch-1—highest grade; the issuer has the strongest possible ability to repay.

Fitch-2—very good grade; the issuer has strong ability to repay.

Fitch-3—good grade; the issuer has satisfactory ability to repay.

Fitch-4—poor grade; the issuer's ability to repay is minimal.

Certificates of deposit ratings

Fitch CD-1 + —strongest degree of assurance for timely payments.

Fitch CD-1—strong degree of assurance for timely payments.

Fitch CD-2—timely payments are assured, but with a lower margin of safety.

Fitch CD-3—satisfactory degree of assurance for timely payments.

Standard & Poor's Corporation supplements its ratings with these signals:

L—the rating applies only to principal, when deposit collateral is fully insured by a federal deposit insurance agency.

*—the rating is contingent upon S&P's receipt of an executed copy of an escrow agreement, confirming investments and cash flows.

N.R.—no rating was requested, or information was not sufficient.

Standard & Poor's also rates corporate and municipal notes and commercial paper:

Notes

SP-1—the issuer has a very strong capacity to repay.

SP-2—the issuer's capacity to repay is satisfactory.

SP-3—the note is speculative.

Commercial paper

A—highest rating; the issuer has the greatest capacity for timely payments.

A-1—the issuer has a very strong capacity for timely payments.

A-2—the issuer has a strong capacity for timely payments.

A-3—the issuer has a satisfactory capacity for timely payments.

B—the issuer has adequate capacity for timely payments.

C—the issuer's capacity for timely payments is doubtful.

D—the issuer is in default or expected to default.

Moody's rates investment grade, short-term municipal notes in a similar manner:

MIG1—highest quality

MIG2—high quality

MIG3—favorable quality

MIG4—adequate quality

Knowing the safety ratings for each bond helps isolate your selection, assuming you have already identified an acceptable level of risk. In comparison with the stock market, the availability of ratings in the bond market makes a decision much easier.

Stocks are not directly rated, although some services do assign safety and timeliness rankings to selected ones. The *Value Line Investment Survey*, for example, reports in detail on 1,700 stocks, ranking them between 1 (highest) and 4 (lowest) in terms of safety of capital and timeliness of purchase. But even with such rankings, stock selection with the safety issue in mind is much more difficult than is bond selection.

junk bond: a bond rated lower than BBB (Baa), also called a "high-yield" bond. Junk bonds are speculative compared with investment grade bonds.

JUNK BONDS

All bonds rated BB (Ba) or lower are in the speculative grade. Collectively, this group is referred to as *"junk" bonds*, although salespeople prefer to call them high-yield bonds. While that may sound better, remember that "high-yield" also means "high-risk."

A bond rated BB (Ba) is considered speculative, and the issuer's ability to repay is not strong. That doesn't mean that you won't be repaid, only that you face more risk with this bond than with a bond rated AAA (Aaa). But a bond rated C is in default or will be soon. The difference between BB and C is substantial.

As of July 1989, investors held $200 billion in corporate junk bonds, compared with only $14 billion in 1984 and $7 billion in 1983. Defaults among junk bond issues between January and September 1989 were $3.2 billion.[2]

A company whose financial strength places its bonds in the lower-than-investment-grade categories may attract investors by adding one or more features to its offering. These include setting up a sinking fund, in which a part of current earnings are set aside each year to protect bond investors from default.

Another way to improve a junk bond's appeal is by giving it a convertible feature. If investors are able to exchange debt securities for equity, that is a form of protection against default. Remember, though, if the corporation is insolvent, it may make little difference whether your investment is debt or equity.

Junk bonds were originally associated with smaller, emerging companies. The higher-than-average yield reflected the company's lack of financial strength, but investors were willing to assume the risks—in the same way that stock investors buy shares of new companies hoping

[2]Source: Gannett News Service, September 24, 1989.

those shares will grow in market value in the future.

In the second half of the 1980s, junk bonds were used increasingly to finance hostile takeovers and leveraged buy-outs. And many mutual funds came into existence just to offer investors a diversified market in junk bonds. The growth in volume of these speculative debt securities led to a substantial market correction in 1989, meaning that many investors found themselves with large paper losses.

This problem demonstrates the importance of identifying an acceptable risk level *before* buying bonds, particularly the speculative variety. It does little good to earn a high yield if you end up with losses from default.

Yellow Sheets: a daily listing of markets in corporate debt securities, published by the National Quotation Bureau.

Blue List: A daily listing of municipal bond issues and ratings published by Standard & Poor's Corporation.

Daily Bond Buyer: A daily publication of the municipal bond industry, reporting statistics and other information on municipal debt securities.

THE FINANCIAL NEWS

Bond ratings and other market information can be found in a number of published sources. These include the *Yellow Sheets*, daily listings of corporate debt securities put out by the National Quotations Bureau; the *Blue List*, a daily listing of municipal bonds published by Standard & Poor's; and the *Daily Bond Buyer*, a publication of the municipal bond industry published each weekday and reporting analytical information.

Each rating service publishes booklets periodically, reporting the current status of the bonds it rates. For example, Fitch Investors Service prints its *Rating Register* every month. Brokers receive these publications, and most are also available by subscription to individual investors.

Financial newspapers and magazines are another source for new bond issues, calls, and issuers' announcements. Daily and weekly financial papers also provide complete bond listings and quotations. Two samples of bond news are shown in Figure 9–2.

The excerpt at the top of the figure tells you the name of the issuer, the amount of the issue, nominal yield, and maturity date. The issuer will also publish an official statement and run an ad giving more details. The excerpt at the bottom is typical of a call announcement. It reports the company's name, nominal yields of the issues involved, call dates, the amount of total debt, and the redemption price.

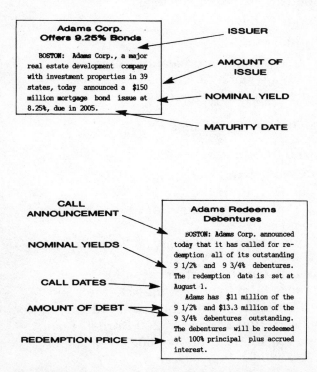

FIGURE 9–2 Sample Bond Issue Announcement (top) and Call (bottom)

Bond listings are broken down into several groups and will include all publicly traded corporate, municipal, and U.S. government debt securities. For example, *Barron's*, a weekly paper, includes the following listings in each of its Monday editions:

- Bonds/Government
    - tax-exempt bonds
    - mortgage-related securities
    - U.S. Treasury bills
    - U.S. Treasury notes and bonds
    - U.S. Treasury zero coupon STRIPS

- Bonds/New York Exchange
- Bonds/Foreign
- Mutual Funds
    - stock, bond, and balanced funds
    - money market funds
    - tax-free money market funds

- Bonds/American Stock Exchange

- Market Laboratory/Bonds
    - weekly bond statistics
    - bond volume
    - bond rating changes for Moody's, Fitch, and S&P
    - other trends and analysis

This is a wealth of information for investors or for those thinking of getting into the bond market. *Barron's* is published every Monday. The subscription address is 200 Burnett Road, Chicopee MA 01021; phone: 800-257-1200 or 800-222-3380 (in Pennsylvania).

For those who want to track the market more frequently than once a week, two daily papers provide the same level of news: the *Wall Street Journal* (same address and phone number as *Barron's*) and *Investor's Daily*, P.O. Box 25970, Los Angeles CA 90025; phone 800-831-2525 or 800-621-7863 (in California).

Additional bond news may be found in a number of financial magazines, including *Fortune, Forbes, Business Week, Financial World, Changing Times,* and *Money*.

Specialized newsletters may also provide analytical and market information. One way to select a newsletter is to buy a limited subscription to several publications at the same time. This can be done through Select Information Exchange (SIE) (2095 Broadway, New York NY 10023), which will send a free catalog of the publications it offers.

HOW BONDS ARE LISTED

Corporate and U.S. government bonds are listed at a percentage of par value. Unless otherwise indicated, the listings refer to par values of $1,000. Thus, if the actual par value is $5,000, the dollar value of a closing price should be multiplied by five. Table 9–A gives examples.

TABLE 9–A   Sample Bond Listings

$1,000 Par:		$5,000 Par:	
Listed Price	Dollar Value	Listed Price	Dollar Value
82	$ 820	82	$4,100
96	960	96	4,800
103	1,030	103	5,150
110	1,100	110	5,500

Par is reported in Roman numeral values, with 'M' representing one thousand. Thus, a bond with a par of $1,000 is summarized as 1M, and if par is $5,000, the listing is summarized as 5M.

Bond prices with fractional values may be listed in eighths, sixteenths, thirty-seconds, or sixty-fourths. These fractional listings appear to the right of the decimal point, and a '+' symbol following the '+' indicates the value is in sixty-fourths.

Examples:

97.12 = 970 plus $^{12}/_{32}$ (or $^3/_8$), which is $3.75
Thus, the total value per $1,000 is:

97	= $970.00
.12	= 3.75
Total	= $973.75

102.27+ = $1,020 plus $^{55}/_{64}$ (.27 without the '+' is $^{27}/_{32}$ or $^{54}/_{64}$, and the '+' tells us that an additional 64th is added. The fractional value of 27+ is $8.59. Thus, the total value is:

102	= $1,020.00
.27+	= 8.59
Total	= $1,028.59

Table 9–B summarizes the value of each fractional value.

Some listings show the current price, but others report yields or percentages of discount being bid or asked. You should understand these distinctions in order to make sense of bond quotations.

READING BOND QUOTATIONS

Corporate bond quotations are similar to quotations for stocks. As illustrated in Figure 9–3, a

TABLE 9–B   Bond Fractional Values

Value Symbol	Fraction	Per $1,000	Value Symbol	Fraction	Per $1,000
+	$1/64$	$0.16	.16+	$33/64$	$ 5.16
.1	$1/32$	0.31	.17	$17/32$	5.31
.1+	$3/64$	0.47	.17+	$35/64$	5.47
.2	$1/16$	0.63	.18	$9/16$	5.63
.2+	$5/64$	0.78	.18+	$37/64$	5.78
.3	$3/32$	0.94	.19	$19/32$	5.94
.3+	$7/64$	1.09	.19+	$39/64$	6.09
.4	$1/8$	1.25	.20	$5/8$	6.25
.4+	$9/64$	1.41	.20+	$41/64$	6.41
.5	$5/32$	1.56	.21	$21/32$	6.56
.5+	$11/64$	1.72	.21+	$43/64$	6.72
.6	$3/16$	1.88	.22	$11/16$	6.88
.6+	$13/64$	2.03	.22+	$45/64$	7.03
.7	$7/32$	2.19	.23	$23/32$	7.19
.7+	$15/64$	2.34	.23+	$47/64$	7.34
.8	$1/4$	2.50	.24	$3/4$	7.50
.8+	$17/64$	2.66	.24+	$49/64$	7.66
.9	$9/32$	2.81	.25	$25/32$	7.81
.9+	$19/64$	2.97	.25+	$51/64$	7.97
.10	$5/16$	3.13	.26	$13/16$	8.13
.10+	$21/64$	3.28	.26+	$53/64$	8.28
.11	$11/32$	3.44	.27	$27/32$	8.44
.11+	$23/64$	3.59	.27+	$55/64$	8.59
.12	$3/8$	3.75	.28	$7/8$	8.75
.12+	$25/64$	3.91	.28+	$57/64$	8.91
.13	$13/32$	4.06	.29	$29/32$	9.06
.13+	$27/64$	4.22	.29+	$59/64$	9.22
.14	$7/16$	4.38	.30	$15/16$	9.38
.14+	$29/64$	4.53	.30+	$61/64$	9.53
.15	$15/32$	4.69	.31	$31/32$	9.69
.15+	$31/64$	4.84	.31+	$63/64$	9.84
.16	$1/2$	5.00	.32	1	10.00

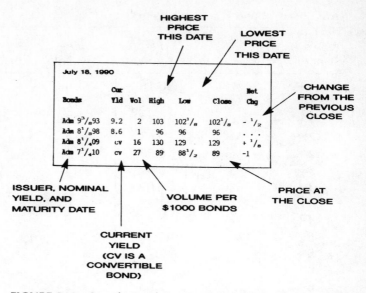

FIGURE 9–3   Sample Bond Quotation from the Financial Press

listing shows the yield, volume, high and low prices, closing price, and change in price. We will track the information shown for our fictitious company, Adams Corporation. The first line reports:

Adm 9⅜9—This identifies one specific bond. The Adams Corporation bonds maturing in 1993 yield 9⅜ percent, or $93.75 per year.

9.2—This is the current yield, which includes an adjustment for the premium reflected in today's price and for the years until maturity.

2—The volume is reported in thousands. Thus, 2,000 bonds traded hands on this date.

103—This was the highest price reached during trading on this date.

102⅛—This was the lowest price reached during trading on this date.

102⅛—This is the day's closing price.

−½—The bond's closing price is ½ of 1 point down from the closing price of the previous trading day. That is a $5.00 change.

A much different quotation is encountered for Treasury bonds and notes. In the first line of the typical quotation illustrated in Figure 9–4, we can find the following information:

10½s—This is the interest rate for the note.

1994—This is the maturity year.

Jan n—January is the month the note will mature. The 'n' tells us this is a note. If there is no symbol, it is a bond.

106.21—The bid is $106^{21}/_{32}$ percent of par. A $1,000 note at this price is worth $1,066.56:

$$106 \quad = \$1,060.00$$
$$^{21}/_{32} \quad = \quad \underline{\quad 6.56}$$

$$\text{Total} = \$1,066.56$$

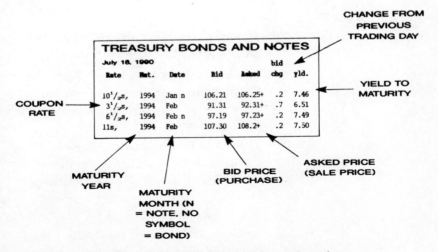

FIGURE 9–4 Sample T-Bond and T-Note Quotation from the Financial Press

"Bid" is the price at which the broker is willing to buy the note.

106.25+—Asked price is 106^{25}/$_{64}$ percent of par. The '+' indicates 64ths rather than 32nds. A $1,000 note at this price is worth $1,063.91:

$$106 \quad = \$1,060.00$$
$$^{25}/_{32} \quad = \quad\underline{\quad 3.91}$$
$$\text{Total} = \$1,063.91$$

"Asked" is the price at which the broker will sell the note.

.2—This is the change from the previous day's bid price. A quote of .2 is ^{2}/$_{32}$ of a point, or $6.25.

7.46—This is the percentage of yield to maturity.

Treasury bill quotations are reported in yet another way. A sample is shown in Figure 9–5. Tracking the first line, we discover the following:

7-23—Maturity month is July, and maturity date is July 23.

5.26—The bid is not a percentage of par, but the percentage of discount from par value. This is the discount the broker is willing to pay to buy the Treasury bill.

5.20—The asked is also a percentage of discount from par. This is the discount the broker offers to sell the Treasury bill.

5.27—This is the annualized yield if the Treasury bill is purchased at the asked price and held until maturity.

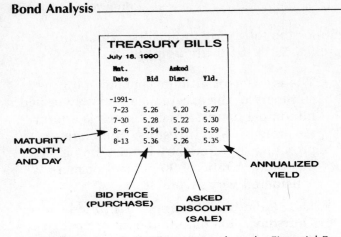

FIGURE 9–5 Sample T-Bill Quotation from the Financial Press

These formats show how various types of bonds are listed in quotations. Like government securities, municipal bonds are shown by bid and asked prices; however, the values in those columns will be percentages of par.

BOND ANALYSIS

Analysts pay close attention to the ratings assigned by Fitch, Moody's, and S&P. In addition, they may judge market sentiment, issuer's strength, and credit status by applying a number of analytical tests. For corporate issues, financial strength is measured by the same criteria used for stock market fundamental analysis: profits, earnings per share, competitive strength, assets, dividends declared and paid, and so forth.

For municipal issues, the same tests cannot be applied. A municipal issuer's strength must be judged on the basis of its ability to generate revenues through taxes or project income. Thus, a different series of analytical tests has been developed for the municipal market. This series in-

placement ratio (acceptance ratio): a statistic included in the *Daily Bond Buyer* summarizing the sentiment of municipal bond buyers. When more than 90 percent of newly issued bonds have been placed (sold), it is considered a favorable trend.

30-day visible supply: a statistic published in the *Daily Bond Buyer* every Thursday reporting on municipal issues coming onto the market in the next 30 days.

20-bond index: a statistic included in the *Daily Bond Buyer* summarizing average yields on highly rated bonds with 20-year maturities.

11-bond index: a sampling taken from the 20-bond index, published in the *Daily Bond Buyer* of the highest-rated bonds with 20-year maturities.

cludes the following indicators, which are published in the *Daily Bond Buyer:*

- The *placement ratio* (acceptance ratio) is a summary of the acceptance of newly issued municipal bonds. "Acceptance" is a term meaning sales to investors. The more promptly investors buy bonds, the better this ratio. A ratio of 90 percent or more is considered very favorable.

- The *30-day visible supply* is printed every Thursday. This reports the municipal issues that will be coming onto the market during the next 30 days.

- The *20-bond index* shows the average yield of bonds with 20-year maturities and in the higher rating groups. Changes in the index are considered indicators of long-term interest rate trends.

- The *11-bond index* is a sampling drawn from the 20-bond index of the highest-rated bonds.

- S&P's "Blue List" includes details of municipal issues, including a test called *floating supply*. This is the total par value amount of all municipal bonds issued.

In judging a municipality's ability to repay its debts, several tests are used as rules of thumb:

- The *25 percent rule* states that a municipality's total debts should not exceed 25 percent of its total revenue budget.

- The *20 percent cushion rule* states that facility revenue should be higher than 20 percent of the budgeted cash payments, which include expenses, maintenance, and debt service on bonds. This creates a 20 percent cushion in case expenses are higher than estimated.

- The *10 percent guideline* sets the standard that the total of a municipality's debt should be 10 percent or less of the market value of real estate in the area.

THE YIELD CURVE

There is a tendency for the yield of a bond to rise during the short term and flatten out as the years to maturity are extended. Analysts study this tendency, which is called the *yield curve*. Changes in the curve reflect the sum of all buying and selling activity between issue and maturity dates, with the yield, price, and risk level all affecting investment decisions.

The yield curve is also affected by the assumed *reinvestment rate* for interest received. Thus, if market rates are higher than the fixed rate on a bond, that bond's yield curve will decline over time as its market value becomes discounted.

Example: A bond pays a nominal rate of 10 percent. During the time the bond is held, the reinvestment rate remains steady at 10 percent. This is a level reinvestment rate, and thus the yield curve, shown in Figure 9–6, is a straight line.

In practice, though, the longer the time until maturity, the greater the chance that the reinvestment rate will grow above the bond's yield. When that rate is greater than yield to maturity, the overall yield curve will flatten out with time. This is called the *normal yield curve*, and it is

floating supply: the total dollar value of outstanding municipal bond issues published in the "Blue List" each day.

25 percent rule: a general rule used by analysts stating that a municipality's debt should not be greater than 25 percent of its total revenue budget.

20 percent cushion rule: a general rule used by analysts stating that the revenue from a facility should be higher than 20 percent of budgeted cash payments, including expenses, maintenance, and debt service. This creates a cushion for unexpected expenses.

10 percent guideline: a general rule used by analysts stating that the total of bonded debt should be 10 percent or less of the market value of real estate in the area.

yield curve: the trend in a bond's total yield, which summarizes the effect of all buying and selling activity. Yield, price, and risk are taken into account. As a general rule, the yield curve rises during the short term and levels out when maturity date is farther away.

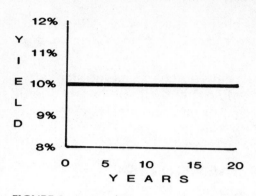

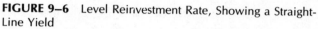

FIGURE 9–6 Level Reinvestment Rate, Showing a Straight-Line Yield

reinvestment rate: the rate at which an investor is able to reinvest income from bond investments.

normal yield curve: a yield curve that rises in the short term and levels out when maturity date is farther away.

shown in Figure 9–7. The curve itself reflects the attitudes of the market as a whole toward a particular bond.

If market rates decline below the bond's fixed rate, then the yield curve will appear opposite of the normal—it will tend to rise rather than flatten out.

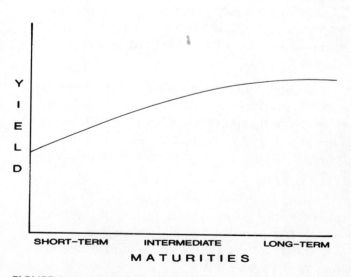

FIGURE 9–7 Normal Yield Curve

You may be able to analyze bonds, read quotations, and gather information. However, the method of buying into the market depends on the issuer and on your personal goals. For example, if you seek diversification but have a limited amount of money to invest, you may decide to buy shares in a bond mutual fund. The next chapter explains how to find the bond market.

10

Finding the Market

Bonds can be purchased in a number of ways: directly from a Federal Reserve Bank or through a dealer (for U.S. government securities); through a brokerage firm (for corporate and municipal issues); or through investment in bond mutual funds.

In this chapter we explain how each of the market outlets for debt securities work and compare the various forms of ownership registration for bonds. We will also explain the benefits of buying shares in a bond mutual fund—such as for diversification and professional management or when you have a limited amount of capital to invest.

THE FEDERAL RESERVE SYSTEM

Trading in U.S. government securities—savings bonds as well as Treasury bills, notes, and bonds

Federal Reserve System (Fed): an agency founded in 1917 to manage federal government banking matters, market government debt securities, regulate the banking industry, and establish monetary policies. The Fed consists of a Board of Governors, 12 Federal Reserve banks, and the Federal Open Market Committee.

Federal Open Market Committee (FOMC): an agency of the Federal Reserve System that buys and sells U.S. government securities.

—is managed by the *Federal Reserve System.* You can buy these securities in a number of ways.

The "Fed" is the government's bank and brokerage firm. Just as a company uses a bank to manage its cash and checking activities, the federal government utilizes the Federal Reserve system to clear checks and to collect its tax revenues. And just as a company interested in issuing a new bond hires an investment banker to underwrite the issue, the Fed serves as the investment banker for newly issued Treasury bills, notes, and bonds.

The Federal Reserve System was founded by Congress in 1917. It consists of a Board of Governors, 12 Federal Reserve banks, and the *Federal Open Market Committee* (FOMC), which manages the actual marketing of newly issued debt securities. (Figure 10–1 illustrates the organization of the Federal Reserve System.)

The Fed provides the following services:

1. *The Board of Governors.* The Board of Governors regulates all member banks in the United States. It also sets reserve requirements.

2. *Federal Reserve banks.* Each of the 12 district banks provides currency and distributes it through other banks; each holds reserve balances of member banks and lends those reserves to members; and each manages the U.S. debt—recording purchases and sales, redeeming matured securities, and collecting and paying funds. The Federal Reserve banks also manage government trust fund portfolios.

3. *Federal Open Market Committee.* This office buys and sells government securities, a function similar to what brokerage firms do for

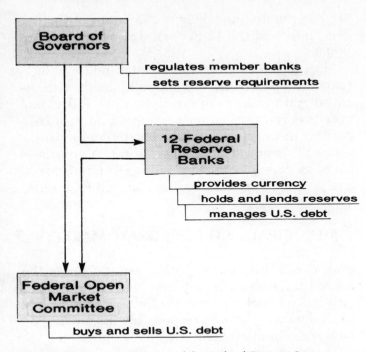

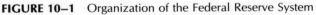

FIGURE 10–1 Organization of the Federal Reserve System

corporations and municipalities that issue
bonds.

The regulatory role of the Fed can be compared with the role of the Securities and Exchange Commission. The SEC regulates activities
in the securities industry under provisions of the
Securities Act of 1933 and the Securities Exchange Act of 1934. Government-issued securities are exempt from SEC jurisdiction, so the Fed
regulates banking practices and protects investors.

Buying and selling through the Federal Open
Market Committee is managed at the New York
Federal Reserve Bank. The FOMC is made up of

the 7 appointed members of the Board of Governors, plus 5 of the 12 Federal Reserve Bank presidents.

Most of the Treasury bills, notes, and bonds issued are purchased at auction by banks and institutional investors in multiple units. Individual investors can then purchase individual debt securities through brokerage firms. In comparison, series EE bonds can be bought through your local bank at any time. And series HH bonds are available only by exchanging matured EE bonds.

MUNICIPAL AND CORPORATE MARKETS

Both municipal and corporate issues come to the market through an investment banker, or underwriter. The lead underwriter forms a syndicate of dealers who will be responsible for moving a new issue to the market.

The municipality or corporation offering a bond enters a contract with the investment banker, acting as underwriter, to market the debt security. The underwriter then enters contracts with syndicate members, which comprise the selling group, and these members then sell investors units of the total issue. The route to the market is shown in Figure 10–2.

A number of dealers will be involved in a syndicate, and the contract may be entered in one of two ways: calling for either shared responsibility for selling the whole issue or individual responsibility for selling a portion of the issue.

An agreement called an *Eastern account* is the most popular. Under terms of this agreement, each member of the syndicate agrees to market a predetermined portion of the total issue. If they

Eastern account: the most popular form of syndication agreement, in which each member is responsible for marketing a specified portion of a new issue. If a firm fails to market its quota, the other firms in the syndicate become responsible for selling the remainder.

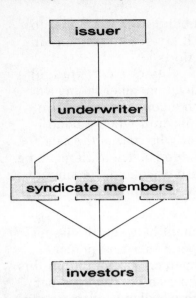

FIGURE 10–2   The Route of a Bond from Issuer to Investors

do not market their entire quota, the remaining members will be responsible for selling any bond units that remain.

A *Western account* is less popular. Under its contract terms, each member of the syndicate is solely responsible for selling a predetermined portion of the issue, and no other members will be held responsible for any unsold portions.

Most municipal issues are contracted through a *competitive bid*. The municipality may be required by its own charter to seek bids and to contract with the underwriting group offering the highest bid price.

Corporations are not required to seek competitive bids and most often enter underwriting agreements through *negotiated bids*. A single underwriting group negotiates the terms and prices with the corporation.

Several layers of participation are involved in

Western account: a version of the syndicate agreement in which each member is responsible only for marketing a specified portion of a new issue. No one firm will be held responsible for marketing unsold units of other members in the syndicate.

competitive bid: a form of bid commonly found in municipal bond offerings. Several underwriting groups bid for the new issue, and the contract is awarded to the group offering the highest bid price.

negotiated bid: a form of contract common for corporate bond offerings. The issuer negotiates terms with a single underwriting group.

getting a newly issued bond from the issuer to the market. And at each layer, the company involved is paid for its efforts.

The issuer (a municipality or a corporation) compensates the syndicate member taking the bond to market through a *concession*. In turn, the syndicate gives a discount when a bond is transferred to the dealer who makes the sale, which is called the *takedown*. The difference between the final purchase price and the amount that ends up in the issuer's hands is called the *spread*.

concession: the compensation paid to syndicate members by the issuer for marketing a new issue.

takedown: the compensation paid to dealers by the syndicator for selling units of a new issue.

spread: the difference between the payment made by the investor for a bond and the amount the issuer receives, consisting of the concession and the takedown.

Example: The agreement between the issuer and the underwriter specifies a 2.50 percent concession and a 5.00 percent takedown. In this case, an investor purchases a bond with a par value of $1,000 through a brokerage firm acting as dealer. The dealer purchased the bond for $995, and the $5 difference is the takedown. The syndicate paid $992.50 to the issuer, so the $2.50 difference is the concession.

The difference between the $1,000 paid by the investor and the $992.50 going to the issuer is the spread:

Paid by the investor	$1,000.00
Less: dealer's takedown	− 5.00
Paid to the syndicate	$ 995.00
Less: syndicate concession	− 2.50
Paid to the issuer	$ 992.50
The spread:	
Paid by the investor	$1,000.00
Received by the issuer	− 992.50
Spread	$ 7.50

The terminology of these stages of payment may vary from one brokerage firm to another. The term "concession" may be applied to the dealer's compensation, and other terms, such as "commission" may also be used.

The levels described above apply to a bond moved to the market through the syndicate. But what if you want to purchase a bond and your broker is not a member dealer in the syndicate? The syndicate contracts with a finite number of dealers, but nonmembers may be able to sell those bonds as well. In that case, the syndicate is bypassed completely, and the issuer receives a greater amount of payment:

Paid by the investor	$1,000.00
Less: nonmember dealer's takedown	− 2.50
Paid to the issuer	$ 997.50

The spread and concession are based on contractual terms arrived at between the underwriter and the issuer, and they are described in terms of "points." There are 100 points per bond, so a $1,000 bond will consist of 100 points, each worth $10.00. For example, a 2.50 percent concession is equal to ¼ point, when $10.00 is equal to one full point. And a 5.00 percent takedown is equal to ½ point. The path of payments, to member and nonmember dealers, is shown in Figure 10–3.

THE OVER-THE-COUNTER MARKET

Most investors are aware that a number of public exchanges list securities. This is especially true of the stock market, which consists of the New York Stock Exchange and a number of other national and regional exchanges acting as outlets for transacting business.

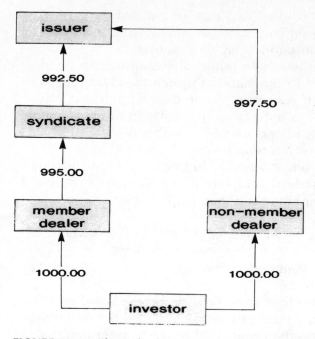

FIGURE 10–3 The Path of Payments Made to Member and Nonmember Dealers

over-the-counter (OTC): a nonexchange market conducted primarily by telephone, on which most bonds are bought and sold. Quotations are accessed via an automated network called the National Association of Securities Dealers Automated Quotations (NASDAQ) system.

In the bond market, the predominant exchange is called the *over-the-counter (OTC)* market. This is a market of dealers who may or may not belong to a securities exchange. They conduct most of their business by telephone. All U.S. government securities, federal agency securities, and municipal bonds are traded over-the-counter, as are most corporate debts. Only a small number of bonds are listed on the New York Stock Exchange.

The OTC market is huge. It includes not only the bulk of debt security transactions, but buy and sell orders in a large number of stocks as well. The market is organized and tracked through the National Association of Securities

Dealers Automated Quotations system, or NAS-DAQ. This system, originated in 1971, is a computerized communications network for dealers, regulators, and investors. Brokers all over the country can obtain quotations for all OTC securities over a desk terminal.

Firms participating in the OTC market are referred to as broker/dealers. They may act in either capacity, but not in both at the same time. As a broker, the firm represents a number of customers, placing business in their behalf. When acting as a broker, the firm is an agent to each customer. It doesn't assume a market risk because it is compensated only for executing a trade; it never owns the securities itself. As a dealer, the firm purchases securities for its own account and then sells them to investors at a marked-up price. When it performs this function, the firm is a principal. The risks are greater for the dealer, since the value of a purchased security may rise or fall on the basis of changes in the market; however, the profit will also be greater from marked-up sales than it would be from earning a commission as broker.

The OTC market is different from the exchange market not only because it isn't located in one place, but because it is a negotiated market with prices set according to marked-up value. The exchange market operates as an auction, with prices based on bid and offered prices.

FORMS OF REGISTRATION

In the unautomated world of the past, investors were given physical possession of a certificate, proving ownership. Today, with transactions

book entry system: the system in use for registration of most bonds sold today. Rather than issuing a certificate of ownership, registration is made by way of entry on an automated system.

registered bond: a bond issued to an identified owner. It may be sold by transfer of ownership and redeemed only by the current registered owner.

bearer bond: a negotiable bond that is issued in nonregistered form. The holder of a bearer bond may redeem it.

registered as to principal only: a bond that is registered so that the owner may redeem it upon maturity but interest is paid to the coupon bearer.

coupon: a slip attached to the bond certificate that is clipped and mailed to the issuer to claim interest payments.

managed for the most part by computer, ownership usually exists on paper only, which is ultimately more efficient.

Even when certificates are issued, most investors don't actually receive them. When handled through a brokerage firm, bonds as well as stocks are commonly registered in "street name." That means the brokerage firm receives the certificates and safeguards them in the investor's behalf.

In the modern method of registration through automated recording rather than by certificate, known as the _book entry system_, the owner's name is recorded on the broker's computer system. This makes it easier and faster to complete a purchase, and it expedites the transfer when a bond is sold, because the authorized sale is made via computer terminal rather than requiring delivery of an endorsed certificate.

Not having to worry about safeguarding bond certificates is practical and convenient. Today, most bonds are registered to a named owner, who is an individual, a couple holding the security in joint tenancy, or a company. These are called _registered bonds_. Some bonds are not registered to a named owner, but are issued in _bearer_ form. Thus, the person in possession of the certificate is assumed to be the owner. A bearer bond is negotiable, since it exists in unregistered form.

With registered bonds, which are far more common than bearer bonds, the owner has rights to interest payments or accruals, as well as to redemption value, in most instances. Two varieties of registered bonds may be found. When a bond is "_registered as to principal only_," the registered owner can redeem the bond at maturity, although interest payments are made to the person who submits the _coupon_. Coupon clipping is not common today, but it was popular in the past.

Bond certificates were issued with a series of
coupons attached, which owners cut off and sent
to the issuer to claim interest twice per year. Today, interest payments are more often made automatically.

The second variation is "*registered as to interest only*." With this form, the registered owner
receives interest payments; however, the bond
can be redeemed at maturity by the bearer.

**registered as to in-
terest only: a bond
that is registered so
that the owner re-
ceives interest pay-
ments, but which
may be redeemed
upon maturity by
the bearer.**

BOND MUTUAL FUNDS

For many investors, purchasing bonds directly
may not be a practical move. First, it may be impossible to diversify a portfolio with a limited
dollar value. Second, a number of bonds (munic-
ipals, for example) are most commonly sold in
five-bond lots, requiring a deposit of $5,000 per
investment. And third, compound interest is not
possible through direct purchase. To achieve a
compounding effect, semiannual interest payments must be reinvested faithfully.

The compounding problem is overcome in
two ways. The first is by purchasing discounted
bonds. The accrual value is based on compounding, so that the initial purchase price is far below face value. The second method is by buying
shares in a bond mutual fund and reinvesting all
income by purchasing additional shares.

A mutual fund is a company that pools investment capital from many small investors and
manages a diversified portfolio of securities.
Funds may specialize in growth or income
stocks, in various types of bonds, in a balance
between stocks and bonds, or in highly specialized investments.

Most mutual funds are not limited to a specified number of shares. The size of their portfo-

open-end fund:
the most common
form of mutual
fund, in which the
total capitalization
is determined by
the number of
investors and the
amounts they in-
vest. Shares are
bought and sold di-
rectly with the
fund's manage-
ment. Share value
represents the cur-
rent market value
of the portfolio.

closed-end fund: a
form of mutual
fund with a set
level of capitaliza-
tion. Shares may be
bought and sold
only between
investors through
an exchange and
not directly with
the fund's manage-
ment. Market value
may be higher or
lower than the
portfolio's book
value, depending
on demand for
shares.

lios is determined by the number of investors who decide to participate and by the amount of money they remit. This is called an *open-end fund*, since total capitalization is not set, so its capital value may move upward or downward. Open-end fund shares are bought and sold directly by the fund management itself. Share value is equal to the current market value of the entire portfolio, plus cash balances the fund is holding.

A lesser-known variety is the *closed-end fund*. The number of shares is limited, meaning that income cannot be reinvested (thus, you cannot compound). The value of shares is determined not so much by the current market value of the portfolio as by demand for the shares on the market. Closed-end fund shares are traded between investors and not with the fund management. Thus, based on demand, the share value could be substantially higher or lower than the current market value of the portfolio.

The share value of an open-end mutual fund is an important test to apply when making the decision to buy. If the fund is well managed, that value should grow with time, just as a stock's individual share value grows in a well-managed company. *Net asset value (NAV)* is the price per share of a mutual fund. It consists of the market value of the portfolio, plus cash balances and minus any liabilities divided by the number of shares currently outstanding (see Figure 10–4).

$$\frac{\text{portfolio value } + \text{ assets } - \text{ liabilities}}{\text{shares outstanding}} = \text{NAV}$$

FIGURE 10–4   Formula for Net Asset Value (NAV)

Example: One open-end fund currently reports the following information:

Portfolio market value	$82,550,000
Cash on hand	$ 3,407,000
Liabilities (redemptions owed and not yet paid)	$ (245,000)
Net	$85,712,000
Number of shares outstanding	3,904,616

net asset value (NAV): a calculation of the current value per share of mutual funds. The combination of the portfolio's current market value, plus cash on hand, less liabilities, is divided by the number of shares currently outstanding.

To compute NAV:

$$\frac{82,550,000 + 3,407,000 - 245,000}{3,904,616} = \$21.95$$

Shares of this mutual fund are worth $21.95 each.

Mutual funds specializing in bonds may be structured so that the portfolio matches the investment goals of different investors. The stated objective of the fund determines the level of risk. For example, bond funds may specialize in:

1. Corporate bonds only
2. Secured bonds only
3. Municipal issues (tax-free)
4. Bonds with specific maturities, also called target funds
5. Bonds with specific safety levels—for example, investment grade only or _below_ investment grade only (junk bond funds)
6. Government debt security funds
7. Convertible bonds only or convertible bonds and preferred stocks
8. Callable bonds only

In addition, some funds combine income objectives (through interest on bonds and dividends on stocks) with growth (through stocks).

They are described as conservative, moderate, or aggressive, terms which may be generalized indicators of risk/reward levels. The real test of a fund's management is made by comparing the historical record—not only for growth in NAV, but for applying a number of other tests, such as:

1. The performance of the fund during positive *and* negative market conditions
2. The size of the fund (A relatively large or small fund may be viewed as advantageous, depending on your own perceptions and investment goals.)
3. The costs and fees involved in buying and holding shares

MUTUAL FUND FEES

Most of us have heard of load and no-load funds. A load fund is one in which investors are charged a fee, commonly 8½ percent, each time shares are purchased. This fee is used to pay a commission to the salesperson who transacts your order. A no-load fund charges no fee, because there is no salesperson and you make purchases directly with the fund.

An ongoing debate among proponents of each type of fund has done little to clarify the choice. Naturally, salespeople who are compensated by commission try to make a strong case in favor of load funds. Others argue that there is no need to pay a commission, since no-load funds have performed historically on a par with load funds.

If you buy shares of a no-load fund, more of your investment dollars go to work for you immediately. However, that doesn't necessarily mean you are better off. You also need to review the management fees and other expenses charged by the fund.

Management fees are assessed as an amount per $100. This is the fee the fund charges for managing the portfolio, and the amount can vary considerably. In addition, some funds charge what is called a 12b-1 fee. This has been allowed since 1980. The 12b-1 is a charge for the expenses of advertising. Nearly half of all mutual fund companies assess this fee.

The load may be charged initially, which is the most common method. For example, you deposit $100, which is broken down as $8.50 for the load and $91.50 invested. One variety is called the deferred sales charge, or "back-end load." In this variety, you are assessed a fee if and when you withdraw funds; however, the fee declines over time. If you hold shares for one year or less, you are assessed five percent. The fee declines by 1 percent per year, so that by the sixth year, there is no deferred charge.

Some funds also charge an "exit fee," a charge for withdrawing money from the fund. The most common exit fee is 1 percent of the amount withdrawn.

If the combination of management, 12b-1, and exit fees in a no-load fund is higher than the combined fees plus loading in a load fund, you could be better off buying shares in the load fund.

Example: You are considering buying shares in one of two funds. One, a no-load fund, has no exit fee and charges expenses of $2.23 per $100. This includes a 12b-1 fee. The other charges an 8½ percent load, no exit fee, and expenses of $0.55 per $100.

When you compare these charges over a ten-

year period, the load fund is less expensive than
the no-load fund. If you invested $1,000 at the
beginning of the ten-year period, total expenses
after ten years would be:

	No-load Fund	Load Fund
Initial sales charge	$ 0	$ 85.00
Expenses, 10 years	201.90	53.66
Total expenses	$201.90	$138.66

This example is based on two assumptions:
one, that expense levels won't change during the
10 years, and two, that the value of the investment won't change either. Both of these assumptions are unrealistic, but the purpose of the
exercise is to compare fees and not to estimate
future growth potential. When you consider that
expenses for either fund could change, the comparison is made on a fair basis.

A comparison of the various fees and charges
has always been difficult, especially since mutual funds have not reported their various fees in
a consistent manner, and some charges may be
buried in the complicated language of various
sections of a prospectus. However, the Securities
and Exchange Commission imposed new rules
for reporting expenses as of January 1988. All
mutual funds must now use the same yield calculations, and the index in a prospectus must
clearly show the location of all sales, management, administrative, and 12b-1 charges.

OTHER FUND VARIETIES

Besides the popular and widely used mutual
fund, some varieties are available for pooled in-

vesting in debt securities. One is the *unit investment trust (UIT)*. Similar to the mutual fund in
some respects, the UIT also has notable differences.

The UIT is a fixed portfolio of bonds or other
debt securities. Like mutual funds, UITs are designed for specific investment objectives; many
buy portfolios of only tax-exempt bonds, for example. The trust is not managed, meaning bonds
are not bought and sold. The portfolio is fixed
and will be liquidated by a series of future maturities. (An exception may arise if a bond's rating is lowered. In that extreme, the trustee may
liquidate the bond prior to maturity to avoid the
risk of future default.)

The UIT maturities may vary as part of the
overall plan. Investors will receive periodic
interest and redemption of each bond in the
portfolio until the trust has been completely liquidated. UIT shares are traded on open exchanges (like mutual fund shares), and they may
be appropriate for the goal of achieving a specified level of future income. Compounding will
be possible only by reinvesting interest and redemption proceeds elsewhere.

Another variety of pooled debt investing is the
money market fund, a form of no-load mutual
fund designed specifically for investing in short-
term debt instruments. Money market funds pay
interest each month, and those proceeds can be
reinvested to achieve a compounding effect.

Most money market funds supply investors
with free checks, which can be used to withdraw funds in specified minimums (usually
$250 or $500). Shares can also be redeemed by
making a written request to the fund's management.

Since money market instruments are usually

unit investment trust (UIT): a trust that purchases a portfolio of bonds and sells units to investors. Bonds are not bought or sold, and investors receive periodic interest and, upon maturity, redemption value. The UIT is not managed actively.

money market fund: a mutual fund designed to invest only in a portfolio of short-term debt instruments of corporations, municipalities, or the U.S. government.

denominated in very large amounts, they have historically been available only to institutional investors. Now, through the fund, the individual with only a small amount of capital can also participate in the money market.

Money market funds (and similar money market accounts offered by many financial institutions) can be used to hold funds temporarily between other investments or to diversify a portfolio.

Purchased directly or through a pooled fund, bonds can be used in various ways to meet your personal financial planning goals. An evaluation of risk, the timing of future goals, and the amount of capital all will dictate which types of debt securities are appropriate—or whether bonds even belong in your portfolio. This is the topic of the next chapter.

11

Bonds in Your Portfolio

Every investor has to make constant, difficult decisions—not only on what to include in a portfolio, but when to change the strategies that worked yesterday. Keeping up with a changing economic environment is not simple. Understanding how changes (like the ever-changing status of market interest rates) affect profitability and risk requires constant research, review, and rethinking.

YOUR RISK TOLERANCE

The decision to include bonds in your portfolio should be based on the degree of risk you are willing to assume. It should also be coordinated with your personal financial goals. To judge risk, compare bonds to other available investments with these points in mind:

1. *Bonds produce a steady income stream.* Most nondiscounted bonds pay interest twice per year. The dates are set by contract and do not change. In comparison, stocks that pay dividends make payments on a regular basis, but the amount of dividend is not fixed. It may be increased, decreased, or even missed, all determined by a decision of the corporation's board of directors.

Discounted bonds do not *pay* interest, but accrue it over the term you own the bond. While this represents a compounded rate of return, it also means you won't receive cash twice per year. And in most instances, you will be taxed on the accrued interest, even though it wasn't received. (An exception to this general rule is Series EE bonds, for which taxes are deferred.)

2. *The market value of bonds can vary.* Some investors compare bonds and stocks and become attracted to the seemingly fixed value of debt securities. The contract specifies that you will receive the full face value of a bond upon maturity. Thus, the ultimate value doesn't change. But during the holding period, a bond's market value may be substantially higher or lower than face value, depending on how that bond's fixed interest rate compares with rates on other debt securities. What this means is that, in the event you decide to sell a bond before maturity, you might have to accept payment below par. This isn't a problem if you know you will hold onto the bond until maturity. But maturity may be a difficult point to pin down, especially if that date isn't due for 20 years.

3. *You cannot compound interest with par-value purchased bonds.* Buying a bond directly, you will be paid one-half the annual nominal yield twice per year. In this system, you do not automatically achieve the benefit of reinvesting and compounding. You have a similar problem with the direct purchase of stocks, since dividends—in most cases—cannot be applied to the purchase of additional fractional shares.

There are several solutions. First, you can reinvest interest payments, at the then prevailing rate, in a savings account, mutual fund, or other investment. Second, you may purchase bonds through a mutual fund and instruct the management to reinvest all interest and redemption values in additional shares. And third, you can purchase discounted bonds, which do produce a compounded yield during the holding period.

4. *You can judge safety of bonds by paying attention to the rating.* An unusual feature of bonds is that the three major rating services assess the financial strength of the issuer. The rating they assign to each bond tells you how safe your money will be. In some cases, a debenture (which is unsecured) with one company will be a safer investment than a secured bond with a different company.

In comparison, it is much more difficult to judge a company in which you are considering buying stock. The financial strength of the issuer is a secondary factor. The most important element affecting market value is how much demand will exist for those shares. While bonds are traded in a negotiated marketplace, stocks are bought and sold in an auction marketplace.

5. *With bond investments, you do not achieve growth of your capital.* Many stock investors are attracted not so much by the dividend rate or even by the current financial strength of the issuer, but by the potential for growth. You will find a company whose stock will grow in value over the next few years very appealing—if growth is appropriate and matches your own goals.

Bonds, however, do *not* achieve growth of capital. They are designed specifically to produce income in the form of interest. Some investment goals are a better match for income than for growth. For example, if it is most important for you to preserve capital and produce a steady and dependable income stream, bonds, not stocks, should probably represent the larger portion of your portfolio.

6. *The life span of a bond is finite.* A bond comes into existence as of a specific date and matures at another specific date. Thus, its life span is defined and limited. In comparison, the stock of a corporation goes on without end, and you can purchase and sell shares whenever you want.

In some respects, the bond's limited life can be an advantage; in other respects, it is inconvenient. For example, if you match bond investments to a specific future goal, you will be able to coordinate maturity dates with that goal. Also, the problem of the finite life is overcome by investing through a bond mutual fund.

7. *Yield and maturity are related.* You may compare different bonds issued by the same company and notice how yields vary according to the number of years to maturity. As a general rule, longer-term maturities are accompanied by higher yields, even when the safety rating is identical to that of a bond with a shorter-term maturity.

If your goals are extremely long-term, you may seek the advantage of a higher rate. But there is a potential trap as well. If you do not want to tie up your capital for more than 10 years, it would be a mistake to invest in bonds maturing in 20 or 30 years. Even though your bonds could be sold at any time, you risk losing capital if the market value becomes discounted in the future.

STARTING A SAVINGS PLAN

Personal goals vary from one investor to another. And just as important to remember is the fact that *your* goals will change over time, depending on your changing income level and economic status, as well as your age, family size and status, personal perceptions, and the amount of money you have available to invest.

The first goal we will consider is that of starting a savings and investment plan. This applies to someone who does not have an investment portfolio or even very much money in a savings account. If this describes you, remember this point: Your savings plan should contain two parts. First is the liquid part, money available to you if you need it for emergencies and unexpected expenses. Second is the fixed part, designed to meet a specific future goal.

Example: You do not currently have a savings account, and you want to begin putting money away each month. Your goal for the moment is to create a reserve equal to six months' salary. You also recognize the importance of maintaining a degree of liquidity.

The way to reach this goal initially may be to start putting a portion of each paycheck into a passbook savings account or money market fund. These are highly liquid investments, meaning that if you need the money, you can get it immediately. Once you have created an adequate initial liquid reserve, you can begin splitting the periodic investments between liquid savings and a longer-term portfolio.

Assuming that the amounts are limited at first, you should establish the fixed portion of your plan by buying in one of two ways:

1. *Bond mutual fund.* This is the best way to achieve diversification as well as compounded returns.

2. *Discounted bonds*—zero coupon or Series EE. Again, you will benefit from compounding between purchase date and maturity, and you will know in advance when the bond will mature.

Starting a savings plan is a relatively short-term goal. For many people, the hardest part is simply getting started, and many families never even make that step. Once you allow room in your budget to put money aside, the task becomes easier. However, in order for the plan to work, you must resolve not to take money out of your savings except for emergencies. That is why part of the portfolio should be left in a very liquid savings account or money market fund— to help you to avoid breaking into the longer-term bond fund or discounted bond investments you make.

BUYING A FIRST HOME

A second goal worth examining with bonds in mind is the purchase of a first home. For anyone who does not own a home, the most difficult hurdle to overcome is saving enough for the down payment. It is frustrating to see home prices rise at a rate that exceeds your level of savings, making it seem impossible to break into this market. However, by diligently putting money aside, the day will come when you can afford that new home.

Bonds can represent at least part of the portfolio established to save for a down payment. The danger here is that you will seek maximum yields, hoping to win the race with ever-growing home purchase prices. Remember that the higher the yield, the greater the risk. It is much more important to achieve a compounded return than to outpace the market. Thus, for this goal, you will want to invest in a bond fund, or you will want to be prepared to reinvest periodic income from all sources as soon as it is received.

The bonds you select (as well as other investments), should be based on the degree of risk you are willing to assume. For example, if you are willing to take very great risks, you may purchase high-yielding bonds that are rated below investment grade.

If you are looking for growth rather than income, you might decide not to include bonds in your portfolio at all and instead place your capital in equities through the stock market. You will want to buy shares in companies offering growth potential, either by direct purchase or in a growth mutual fund. If you choose the latter, you can select a conservative, moderate, or aggressive growth fund.

SAVING FOR COLLEGE EDUCATION

Another goal shared by many families is saving for a child's college education. For example, you have a child who is now three years old. You have 15 years until that child will be of college age. Bonds are an excellent vehicle for reaching this goal and you can defer taxes by buying certain bonds or by using the tax laws to your advantage. You can also coordinate maturity dates to correspond with annual tuition periods.

With certain restrictions, you can establish a trust, start an Individual Retirement Account (IRA), invest through a tax-deferred annuity, or make a gift to your child, all using bonds and bond funds as the investment of choice. The maturities can also be coordinated with a very specific future date in mind. In order to set up these investments in compliance with tax rules, you should consult with a tax expert.

The other point concerning saving for a college education: Your investment choice should be a very safe one. You don't want to speculate and risk not having enough in value, or you may have to borrow money and create a financial hardship for yourself in the future. Thus, you will want to buy shares in a very conservative bond fund, invest strictly in U.S. government securities, or buy only those bonds with investment-grade ratings.

STARTING YOUR OWN BUSINESS

A large portion of the employed working force has dreams of one day opening an independent small business. A major obstacle, of course, is capital. The security of a regular paycheck, not to mention the valuable benefits paid by an employer, is difficult to ignore. For many, the only way to reach this goal, even if it means having to wait many years, is to begin investing money today so that their goals will be reached in the

future because income is generated from a portfolio.

Bonds may play a part in this financial goal, if
only to create a foundation of income. However,
those who are willing to seriously consider assuming the risks of self-employment may also
have the temperament for riskier investing. They
may end up putting their capital into aggressive
growth stocks and other speculative investments
rather than settling for the relative consistency
and safety of bonds.

We cannot characterize all would-be entrepre-
neurs in this manner, of course. Everyone is
different, and investors should match their
investment philosophy to their own risk tolerance level. For some people, the goal of starting
a new business is not seen as a mid-career, dras-
tic change filled with risk. Instead, it is viewed
as a step to take much later, in combination with
financial security and semiretirement.

Example: You may want to work only 20
hours per week and spend the other 20 hours in
a relatively low-risk business of your own. Many
full-time employees have made this transition as
a step toward retirement—rather than retiring
completely all at once.

THE RETIREMENT GOAL

Achieving a comfortable retirement is a concern
for everyone. The younger you are when you begin planning for retirement, the easier it is to
achieve that goal. However, two points prevent
many people from beginning their retirement
plan while they are still in their twenties or thir-
ties. First is the economic limitation: Many peo-

ple can barely afford to live on their incomes while still building a career. Second is the fact that retirement may seem a distant, intangible event, with other, more immediate goals having a higher priority. Those just starting their careers are not likely to look far ahead and plan for their later years.

The goal is not simply to create a lump sum in preparation for retirement, but to create the conditions for a *comfortable* life-style in retirement. If you depend solely on your employer's pension plan and Social Security, you might not be able to achieve the financial freedom you envision in the future—or even to retire completely. Another question is whether you will want to retire at all. You may plan to continue working past retirement age. However, that assumes that your motivation to work won't change and that your health will permit you to continue working.

A realistic point of view is that, no matter how you feel about working today, it is smart to put some money aside for later years. This can be achieved in a tax-deferred environment in several ways. You can invest up to $2,000 in an Individual Retirement Account, and if you do not participate in another retirement plan (such as the one offered by your employer), you can deduct your IRA contributions from your gross income and avoid taxes on it. Even if you do not qualify for tax deductions, all income you earn in the IRA is tax-deferred.

Self-employed people have a similar advantage through their Keogh plans. These come in variations, but most allow the self-employed person to deposit 25 percent of his or her net profits each year, up to a maximum of $30,000 per year.

For example, if you earn $40,000 in net profits from your own business, you can put $10,000 into a Keogh plan. The entire deposit is deducted from gross income and no taxes are paid. All earnings in your Keogh are deferred, and taxes are paid only when you withdraw funds.

Within an IRA or Keogh, you can invest in a number of different equity and debt securities. If you want to diversify your holdings, you have two choices. Either set up your retirement account with a mutual fund family (a company offering several different funds) and invest in shares of equity and debt funds, or establish a self-directed account and diversify on your own. For example, in a self-directed plan, you can buy shares of stock as well as bonds (both par and discounted). You may also put some of your retirement money into mutual fund shares.

BUILDING CAPITAL OVER TIME

In the management of your portfolio, whether taxable or tax-deferred (through a retirement account), your goal and level of risk tolerance should be kept in mind at all times. In defining these important standards, you may need to work with a qualified professional adviser, such as a certified financial planner. Or, if you are willing to perform your own research, you can make your own decisions and create the capital levels you need and want in the future.

Make a distinction between short-term and long-term goals. You may define "short-term" as only one year or as long as five years. Everyone has a different idea of short-term. Long-term, though, is more specific. For most people, long-term is the time required to meet their distant goals (owning a home, starting a business, retiring).

Your short-term goals should include the need to build an adequate emergency reserve fund. This should be a fund available for you to pay unexpected bills or to help you get through a difficult period when other income ceases. For example, you may lose your job and not be able to find another one for three months. In that event, you would need to build an emergency reserve fund equal to at least three months' income.

Other short-term goals might include just getting a plan off the ground. This may be a problem of budgeting, that is, starting to put money away on a regular basis, as a matter of habit, and allowing it to continue accumulating.

Long-term goals, to be achieved, should contain several elements:

1. They should be specific. For example, your goal may be to save a down payment for a home. But you should also establish the amount you will need in order to make the goal specific.

2. They should have a deadline. For example, knowing how much you need to save to reach your goal is only half the challenge. When will you reach the goal? That defines how much you will need to save, starting today.

3. They should be coordinated with the yield or growth you expect to achieve. For example, you know how much you need to save and when you plan to reach your goal. But what will the yield be, and will it be compounded? Using a book of compound interest tables, you will be able to figure out how your investments will

grow each year on the basis of an assumed rate
of return.

4. They should be started with an eye on the
risk element. Avoid the mistake of investing in a
way that exceeds your risk tolerance standards
just because your goal dictates that you should.
For example, in order to reach your goal (based
on what you can afford to invest today), you will
have to seek investments that yield 11 percent or
more. However, the only way to achieve that
rate is to take risks you don't want to take.

The alternative: Extend the deadline on your
goal and respect your own risk tolerance level,
or accept the limitations of today's income and
plan to modify your goal in the future, when
your income rises. You don't have to base the
success or failure of your long-term goal strictly
on what you can afford to do today. Your long-
term plan can include increasing the amount of
money you save or invest in the future.

DIVERSIFYING YOUR PORTFOLIO

You can diversify your investments in a number
of ways. For example, simply buying shares in a
mutual fund achieves significant diversification
because the total fund portfolio is itself diversified.

You may select a fund with diversification in
mind. Some funds strike a balance between
growth and income. They seek stocks paying
higher-than-average dividends and investment-
grade bonds with competitive interest rates. This
combination achieves the income side. At the
same time, the fund invests in stocks that, in the
opinion of the fund's management, will grow in

value over time. This achieves the growth objective of the fund and helps you to diversify.

You may also divide your portfolio on your own by buying shares in a money market fund as well as in growth and income funds. That provides diversification on two levels. First, each fund is diversified itself. Second, your portfolio is split not only into growth and income, but into short-term and long-term income areas as well.

If you purchase directly, you may diversify by buying both stocks and bonds, or by buying bonds that vary by maturity and risk level. U.S. government securities, for example, are considered the safest investment, since they are guaranteed by the full faith and credit of the United States. Corporate and municipal bonds vary in degrees of safety, dictated by collateral as well as the safety and risk rating assigned to each.

Diversification can be defined in terms of liquidity and term to maturity. A savings account is highly liquid, while a directly purchased bond may become discounted in market value (meaning it can be sold, but only at a loss). You can diversify by selecting bonds with varying maturities, so that your portfolio doesn't turn over too often or remain fixed for too long.

Like any investment, bonds contain attractive features as well as significant limitations. The degree of risk is determined not only by how secure your money is, but by the nature of your own investing goals. It is not appropriate to tie up your money in a 30-year bond if you will need those funds in 15 years. And if you are trying to build a secure foundation paying regular income, it would be a mistake to buy speculative investments, whether debt or equity.

Whether bonds belong in your portfolio is a

matter of individual decision. And that decision should begin with investigation. The more you understand about bonds, the greater your success will be as an investor. Those who make decisions on the basis of information are less likely to err than those who depend on the advice of others or who invest on the basis of generalized (and often wrong) perceptions about risk, safety, and yield.

The knowledge you acquire about bonds, combined with your understanding of your own risk tolerance and your specific goals, is the key. As a well-informed investor, you will be able to select investments that meet your goals and investing standards. Ultimately, you will meet the goal we all have in common: to achieve financial independence and security for your future.

Glossary

acceptance ratio a method for judging the market for bonds. The volume of bonds sold during a period is compared with the level of bond issues available. The higher the ratio, the higher the market acceptance.

accreted interest the method of crediting interest earned on a zero coupon bond (see Figure G–1). Rather than paying interest twice per year, the bond increases its current market value by a level representing the compound yield.

$$\frac{\text{accreted}}{\text{interest}} = \frac{\text{purchase}}{\text{price}} \times \left(1 + \frac{\text{semiannual}}{\text{rate}} \right)^{n} - \frac{\text{purchase}}{\text{price}}$$

FIGURE G–1 Formula for Accreted Interest

accrual the periodic recognition of profit from a bond discount, with equal portions added in each year in the term. The formula for accrual is shown in Figure G–2.

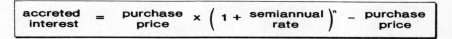

$$\frac{\text{discount amount}}{\text{years}} = \frac{\text{annual}}{\text{accrual}}$$

FIGURE G–2 Formula for Annual Accrual

accumulation the gradual increase in the value of a discounted bond throughout the holding period. Figure G–3 shows how to calculate accumulation.

$$\text{current value} + \text{interest accrual} = \text{annual accumulation}$$

FIGURE G–3   Formula for Annual Accumulation

active bond a bond that trades frequently in high volume and for which demand is high.

aftermarket *see* **secondary market.**

amortization the periodic recognition of loss from a bond premium, with equal portions subtracted in each year in the term. Figure G–4 gives the formula.

$$\frac{\text{premium amount}}{\text{years}} = \text{annual amortization}$$

FIGURE G–4   Formula for Annual Amortization

as agent the status of an investment banker who promises to market as much of the issue as possible (a "best efforts" agreement).

as principal the status of an investment banker who purchases an entire bond issue and then resells units to investors.

bank quality *see* **investment grade.**

banker's acceptance a letter of credit issued by a financial institution to finance transactions between the delivery date and the payment date.

bearer bond a negotiable bond that is issued in nonregistered form. The holder of a bearer bond may redeem it.

Blue List A daily listing of municipal bond issues and ratings published by Standard & Poor's Corporation.

bond a debt obligation issued by a corporation or other issuer, promising to pay periodic interest and to return loaned capital upon maturity. Maturity occurs five or more years from the issue date.

bond anticipation note (BAN) a mortgage note pledged by future bond proceeds.

bond ratio a comparison measuring outstanding bonds as a percentage of total capitalization (see Figure G–5); the ratio may exclude bonds with maturities of one year or less.

$$\frac{\text{outstanding bonds}}{\text{total capitalization}} \ = \ \text{bond ratio}$$

FIGURE G–5 Formula for Bond Ratio

bond yield table a table summarizing yield to maturity for bonds. One table is used for each nominal yield. The first column shows the price of the bond, and other columns show YTM for various maturities.

bonds with warrants attached corporate bonds, usually senior debts, with which investors gain the right, through subscription warrants, to purchase a specified number of shares of the issuer's common stock.

book entry system the system in use for registration of most bonds sold today. Rather than issuing a certificate of ownership, registration is made by way of entry on an automated system.

breakeven interest the amount of interest an investor must earn to break even after income taxes and after inflation. To compute, divide the assumed inflation rate by the after-tax rate (see Figure G–6).

$$\frac{\text{inflation rate}}{100 - \text{tax rate}} \ = \ \frac{\text{breakeven}}{\text{interest}}$$

FIGURE G–6 Formula for Breakeven Interest

call feature a feature written into some bond indentures giving the issuer the right to redeem all or part of the issue prior to scheduled maturity date.

call loan a short-term loan made by a bank to a securities broker-dealer, which may be called with as little as one day's notice.

call protection the period of time between issue date and the first possible call date.

callable bond a bond containing a call feature.

capital gain profit realized when an investment or asset is sold at a price above its cost. When a bond is purchased at a discount and then redeemed at par, the difference is a capital gain.

capital loss a loss realized when an investment or asset is sold at a price below its cost. When a bond is purchased at a premium and then redeemed at par, the difference is a capital loss.

capital market descriptive of bonds issued by governments and corporations with maturities of one year or more from issue date; also stocks and mortgages. Capital market instruments fund the intermediate and long-term growth of business.

capitalization the invested funds available to a company, representing all classes of capital stock, surplus, retained earnings (equity capital), and long-term debt (bonds).

cash management bill a Treasury bill issued irregularly and with a maturity other than 13, 26, or 52 weeks.

CATS Certificate of Accrual on Treasury Securities.

certificates of deposit (CD) debt instruments issued by financial institutions, which mature between seven days and five years, in denominations of $1 million or more.

closed-end the status of property pledged as collateral, when the same property may be pledged for subsequent debts on a subordinated basis.

closed-end fund a form of mutual fund with a set level of capitalization. Shares may be bought and sold only between investors through an exchange and not directly with the fund's management. Market value may be higher or lower than the portfolio's book value, depending on demand for shares.

collateral trust bond a corporate bond secured with the pledge of securities held in trust.

commercial paper an unsecured note issued by a corporation, with maturities from 3 to 270 days, used to provide operating funds when accounts receivable balances are outstanding.

competitive bid a form of bid commonly found in municipal bond offerings. Several underwriting groups bid for the new issue, and the contract is awarded to the group offering the highest bid price.

concession the compensation paid to syndicate members by the issuer for marketing a new issue.

construction bond (completion bond) a corporate mortgage bond for property under construction.

conversion premium the difference between a bond's market value and its conversion value, divided by conversion value (see Figure G–7). It is expressed as a percentage representing an estimate of investors' perception about the convertible bond's current value.

$$\frac{\text{market value} - \text{conversion value}}{\text{conversion value}} = \frac{\text{conversion}}{\text{premium}}$$

FIGURE G–7 Formula for Conversion Premium

conversion price the price per share at which a bond may be converted to common stock, specified in the indenture or computed by dividing the bond's par value by the conversion ratio, as shown in Figure G–8.

$$\frac{\text{par value}}{\text{conversion ratio}} = \frac{\text{conversion}}{\text{price}}$$

FIGURE G–8 Formula for Conversion Price

conversion privilege the bondholder's right to exchange the debt position of a bond for an equity position in the issuer's common stock.

conversion ratio the number of shares to be received upon conversion, specified in the indenture or computed by dividing the bond's par value by the conversion price. The formula is given in Figure G–9.

$$\frac{\text{par value}}{\text{conversion price}} = \frac{\text{conversion}}{\text{ratio}}$$

FIGURE G–9 Formula for Conversion Ratio

conversion value the current market value of common stock, based on the conversion ratio of a bond. It is computed by multiplying the conversion ratio by the stock's current value per share (see Figure G–10).

$$\frac{\text{conversion}}{\text{ratio}} \times \frac{\text{market}}{\text{value}} = \frac{\text{conversion}}{\text{value}}$$

FIGURE G–10 Formula for Conversion Value

convertible bond a corporate bond, usually a junior subordinated debenture, that can be exchanged for shares of the issuer's common stock.

convertible preferred stock a class of preferred corporate stock that can be exchanged for a specified value in common stock.

cooling-off period a period between filing of a bond's registration statement and the first date the issue may be offered to the public. This period is normally 20 days.

coupon a slip attached to the bond certificate that is clipped and mailed to the issuer to claim interest payments.

coupon yield _see_ **nominal yield.**

cover the degree to which a bond issuer is able to honor debt commitments through earnings and cash flow.

current income profits realized during the period an investment is held. Examples include bond interest and stock dividends. In comparison, a capital gain or loss represents the difference between purchase and sale price.

current market value the market value of a bond today, which may be at a premium (above face value) or a discount (below face value).

current yield the yield on a bond based on current market value; more accurate than nominal yield because it is based not on face value, but on value of the bond in today's market. The calculation is shown in Figure G–11.

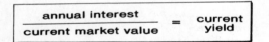

$$\frac{\text{annual interest}}{\text{current market value}} = \begin{array}{c}\text{current}\\\text{yield}\end{array}$$

FIGURE G–11 Formula for Current Yield

Daily Bond Buyer A daily publication of the municipal bond industry, reporting statistics and other information on municipal debt securities.

dated date (issue date) the date when interest begins to accrue on a newly issued bond.

debenture an unsecured corporate debt backed only by goodwill and reputation.

debt capital that portion of capital represented by debt obligations and excluding all forms of equity.

debt security an investment in which capital is loaned to a corporation, government, government agency, or other issuer.

default risk the risk that an issuer will delay or fail to make interest or principal payments as promised, or that the full amount will not be paid on the promised date.

discount the current market value of a bond less than 100; a bond currently valued below face, or par, value (see Figure G–12).

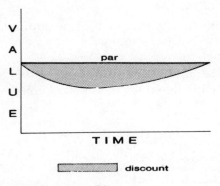

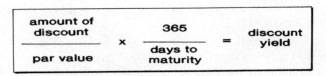

FIGURE G–12 Discount

discount yield (equivalent bond yield) a method of computing the yield on Treasury securities shown in Figure G–13, based on par value rather than on the discounted purchase price.

$$\frac{\text{amount of discount}}{\text{par value}} \times \frac{365}{\text{days to maturity}} = \text{discount yield}$$

FIGURE G–13 Formula for Discount Yield

diversification risk the risk that capital will be placed in a narrow range of investment choices, so that an adverse market condition will affect the entire portfolio; or the risk that a portfolio's average yield will be low due to an overly broad mix of yields and risks.

Eastern account the most popular form of syndication agreement, in which each member is responsible for marketing a specified portion of a new issue. If a firm fails to market its quota, the other firms in the syndicate become responsible for selling the remainder.

11-bond index a sampling taken from the 20-bond index, published in the *Daily Bond Buyer*, of the highest-rated bonds with 20-year maturities.

equipment trust bond a corporate bond issued to purchase capital assets and secured by those assets.

equity capital that portion of capital represented by stockholders' equity and excluding all debt obligations.

equity security an investment in which a portion of ownership is exchanged for money invested, usually represented by shares of stock.

equivalent taxable yield a calculation that compares the after-tax yield of a taxable bond to the yield offered on a municipal bond. The calculation is shown in Figure G–14.

$$\frac{\text{municipal bond yield}}{1 - \text{tax rate}} = \begin{array}{c}\text{equivalent}\\ \text{taxable yield}\end{array}$$

FIGURE G–14 Formula for Equivalent Taxable Yield

face value (par value) the full amount the issuer promises to pay an investor upon maturity of a debt security; a market value of 100.

federal funds reserve balances in excess of requirements on deposit at a Federal Reserve bank.

Federal Open Market Committee (FOMC) an agency of the Federal Reserve System that buys and sells U.S. government securities.

Federal Reserve System (Fed) an agency founded in 1917 to manage federal government banking matters, market government debt securities, regulate the banking industry, and establish monetary policies. The Fed consists of a Board of Governors, 12 Federal Reserve banks, and the Federal Open Market Committee.

final prospectus the full disclosure document that must be given to all investors in newly issued bonds, required by terms of the Securities Act of 1933. The prospectus explains the amount of the issue, maturity date, interest rate and payment dates, the trustee's name and address, and the type of collateral.

financial planning the process of managing investment funds and money-related matters for the purpose of achieving well-defined future goals; the plan is based on complete definition, discipline, and consistency.

first mortgage bond a bond secured by a pledge of real property and holding seniority of claim to that property in the event of default.

floating debt the total of a municipality's debts that will mature within five years or less.

floating supply the total dollar value of outstanding municipal bond issues published in the "Blue List" each day.

funded debt the total of a municipality's debts that will mature beyond five years.

general mortgage bond a bond secured by a pledge of real property with equal or subordinated claim with other creditors in the event of default.

general obligation bond a municipal bond secured by the taxing power of the issuer, also called a full faith and credit bond.

goal a short-term or long-term result planned for by selection of investments and identification of acceptable risks.

inactive bond a bond that trades infrequently, in a thin, or narrow market, for which demand is low.

indenture the agreement entered between the corporation (issuer) and the investor (creditor). All terms of the agreement are specified, including the total of the bond issue, maturity date, interest rate and payment dates, and the trustee's name and address.

indications of interest tentative reservations of bond units made by investors prior to expiration of the cooling-off period.

inflation risk (purchasing power risk) the risk that yield from investments will not keep pace with the rate of inflation; the loss of real purchasing power based on changes in prices and yields.

interest rate risk the risk that prevailing rates will be higher than the rate earned from a fixed-income investment, or a decline in current market value due to changes in interest rates.

interpolation a method for estimating yield to maturity when nominal yield is fractional and not reported in bond yield tables. The YTMs for yields above and below the nominal rate are added together and averaged, as shown in Figure G–15.

$$\frac{\text{yield above} \;+\; \text{yield below}}{2} = \text{interpolated yield}$$

FIGURE G–15   Formula for Interpolated Yield

inverted scale the scale of a serial bond when shorter-term yields are higher than longer-term yields.

investment banker a securities broker-dealer or other firm that organizes the marketing activities for the public offering of a bond.

investment grade (bank quality) a bond with a rating between AAA (Aaa) and BBB (Baa). Ratings below this range are speculative grades.

investment market the complete range of debt and equity instruments used to finance the capital requirements of government and business, including the money market and the capital market.

investment objective the identification of attributes associated with an investment or investment strategy, designed to isolate and compare risks, define acceptable levels of risk, and match investments with personal goals.

investment value an estimate set by a bond analyst of what a convertible bond's lowest likely market value would be without the conversion privilege, assuming that market interest rates remain stable.

issue date the date a bond or other debt security is first placed on the market, which also identifies the time from which interest begins to be earned.

junior security a bond or other debt security with a subordinated claim in the event of default.

junk bond a bond rated lower than BBB (Baa), also called a "high-yield" bond. Junk bonds are speculative compared with investment grade bonds.

leverage a method of investing in which capital is used to gain control over additional funds.

leverage risk the risk associated with borrowing funds to invest. This requires the generation of income adequate to continue repayments of principal and interest, accompanying the opportunity for higher income and growth from a higher level of investment.

limited tax bond a general-obligation bond restricted by the issuer's taxing power. Additional taxes may not be raised to meet the obligation.

liquidity risk the risk that it will not be possible to close an investment position without also accepting a loss.

market risk the risk that a bond's price will change on the basis of supply and demand factors, rating of the issuer's financial strength, and market interest rates.

marketability descriptive of an investment for which an active secondary market exists, making it possible to find another buyer (the public stock and bond exchanges, for example); or an investment in which closing a position does not require finding another buyer (for open-end mutual funds or demand savings accounts, for example).

marketable security a security that is traded publicly, directly with other investors through the exchange market.

maturity date the date a bond or other debt security becomes due; the date an issuer promises to repay investors' capital.

money market descriptive of various forms of debt obligations issued by governments and corporations for which maturity is short term—one year or less from date of issue.

money market fund a mutual fund designed to invest only in a portfolio of short-term debt instruments of corporations, municipalities, or the U.S. government.

moral obligation bond a bond issued with a promise to make repayment even if revenue is insufficient.

mortgage bond a corporate bond secured with the pledge of real property.

negotiated bid a form of contract common for corporate bond offerings. The issuer negotiates terms with a single underwriting group.

net asset value (NAV) a calculation of the current value per share of mutual funds. As shown in Figure G–16, the combination of

$$\frac{\text{portfolio value} + \text{assets} - \text{liabilities}}{\text{shares outstanding}} = \text{NAV}$$

FIGURE G–16 Formula for NAV

the portfolio's current market value, plus cash on hand, less liabilities, is divided by the number of shares currently outstanding.

net yield the yield from a bond after deducting a portion of total income for federal and state income tax liabilities.

New York Plan an infrequently used method for securing collateral for an equipment trust bond, with purchase made by way of installment purchase.

nominal yield (coupon yield) the stated interest rate paid on a bond, computed by dividing the amount of annual income by the bond's par value (see Figure G–17).

$$\frac{\text{annual income}}{\text{par value}} = \text{nominal yield}$$

FIGURE G–17 Formula for Nominal Yield

nonmarketable security a government debt security that cannot be traded publicly, but must be purchased and redeemed through the Federal Reserve system or through the U.S. Treasury.

normal scale the scale of a serial bond when shorter-term yields are lower than longer-term yields.

normal yield curve a yield curve that rises in the short term and levels out when maturity date is farther away. Figure G–18 shows this curve.

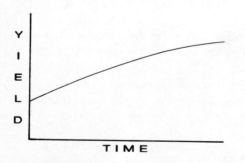

FIGURE G–18 Yield Curve

note a debt obligation similar to a bond, but with a maturity date less than five years from date of issue.

offering date the date a newly issued bond is offered for sale, which may be as many as 30 days prior to dated, or issue date.

official statement a summary of a bond issue's terms: amount, maturity date, interest rate, and trustee.

open-end the status of property pledged as collateral when the priority of claim is equal with the pledge of the same property for other debts.

open-end fund the most common form of mutual fund, in which the total capitalization is determined by the number of investors and the amounts they invest. Shares are bought and sold directly with the fund's management. Share value represents the current market value of the portfolio.

open-market purchase one method of retiring all or part of a bond issue, in which the corporation purchases its own bonds on the open market at current market price.

original issue discount the method under which most U.S. government securities are issued. Investors buy debt securities at a discount and accrue interest during the holding period. Upon maturity, the investor receives par value.

overall debt to market value a ratio comparing a municipality's total debt obligations to actual current market value of real property in the area (see Figure G–19).

$$\frac{\text{overall debt}}{\text{market value}} = \frac{\text{overall debt to}}{\text{market value}}$$

FIGURE G–19 Formula for Overall Debt to Market Value

over-the-counter (OTC) a nonexchange market conducted primarily by telephone, on which most bonds are bought and sold. Quotations are accessed via an automated network called the National Association of Securities Dealers Automated Quotations (NASDAQ) system.

paper any short-term debt security.

par value *see* **face value.**

parity the market price of a convertible bond at which the bond and the common stock of the issuer are identical in market value, shown in Figure G–20.

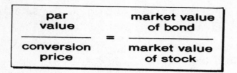

FIGURE G–20 Formula for Parity

per capita debt a ratio comparing a municipality's total debt to the population in the area, shown in Figure G–21.

FIGURE G–21 Per Capita Debt

phantom interest interest that is taxable each year but not received in cash.

Philadelphia Plan the most common method for securing collateral for an equipment trust bond. The trustee holds title until the bond has been retired.

placement ratio (acceptance ratio) a statistic included in the *Daily Bond Buyer*, summarizing the sentiment of municipal bond buyers. When more than 90 percent of newly issued bonds have been placed (sold), it is considered a favorable trend.

preliminary prospectus (red herring) a document similar to the registration statement, but intended for investors who may want to file an indication of interest. It is called a "red herring" because disclosures made on the front page are in bright red ink.

premium the current market value of a bond greater than 100; a bond currently valued above face, or par, value (see Figure G–22).

premium over investment value the percentage difference between market value and investment value, divided by investment value; the current value of the conversion privilege. The formula is given in Figure G–23.

present value the value today of a future sum, assuming a rate of interest, compounding method, and number of periods (see Figure G–24).

primary market the market on which newly issued securities are traded, including government security auctions and underwriting purchases of blocks of new issues, which are then resold.

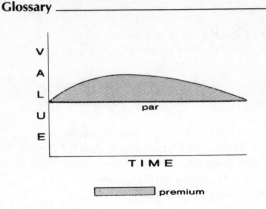

FIGURE G–22   Premium

$$\frac{\text{market value} - \text{investment value}}{\text{investment value}} = \frac{\text{premium over investment value}}{}$$

FIGURE G–23   Formula for Premium over Investment Value

$$\frac{\text{maturity value}}{(1 + \text{half-year rate})^n} = \text{present value}$$

FIGURE G–24   Formula for Present Value

priority (1) the right of certain parties to be paid before other creditors or owners in the event of liquidation and default. (2) the sequence in which debts will be honored when the same property is pledged as collateral for different debts.

professional method a precise method for interpolating yield to maturity. Rather than averaging yields reported above and below the nominal yield, the interval between yields is calculated.

purchasing power risk *see* **inflation risk.**

red herring *see* **preliminary prospectus.**

redemption the repayment of face value of a bond upon maturity.

refunding one method of retiring a bond issue, in which previous bonds are replaced with newly issued ones.

registered as to interest only a bond that is registered so that the owner receives interest payments, but which may be redeemed upon maturity by the bearer.

registered as to principal only a bond that is registered so that the owner may redeem it upon maturity but interest is paid to the coupon bearer.

registered bond a bond issued to an identified owner. It may be sold by transfer of ownership and redeemed only by the current registered owner.

registration statement a disclosure document the issuer is required to file with the Securities and Exchange Commission (SEC) for a bond issue. The statement describes the terms of the bond, including collateral pledged, maturity date, interest rate and payment dates, and the trustee's name and address.

reinvestment rate the rate at which an investor is able to reinvest income from bond investments.

reinvestment risk the risk that it might not be possible to invest interest and principal to earn yields comparable to a bond; that opportunities will be missed because capital is committed to a low-yielding fixed-income investment; or that investors will be unable to compound their returns from bonds.

repurchase agreement (repo) an agreement to sell securities and to repurchase them at a specified price and on a specified future date (often the next day). The repo is used to borrow money invested in securities.

revenue anticipation note (RAN) a mortgage note pledged by future project or facility revenues.

revenue bond a municipal bond issued by an agency, authority, or district and secured by future revenues derived from operation of a facility.

reverse repurchase agreement an agreement to buy securities and to resell them at a specified price and on a specified future date, with interest. The reverse repo is used to deliver securities that have been sold short.

safety ratings a rating of bonds by one of three organizations: Fitch Investors Service, Moody's Investors Service, and Standard & Poor's Corporation.

scale a summary of maturity dates, principal amounts, interest rates, and prices of a serial bond.

secondary market the market on which bonds, stocks, and other investments are traded after the initial offer of securities; the public exchanges.

Securities and Exchange Commission (SEC) an organization that regulates the securities industry, created by provisions of the Securities and Exchange Act of 1934.

selection risk the risk that investment decisions will be based on the isolated basis of yield, name recognition, fundamentals, or general perceptions—to the exclusion of other valid measurements of risk.

selling group the broker-dealers who sell bonds to investors, contracted by the underwriting syndicate.

senior lien an obligation that must be satisfied before other, junior liens. Example: bond obligations are senior to the rights of preferred and common stockholders.

senior security a bond or other debt security with priority of claim in the event of default.

serial bond a bond issued in periodic segments with varying maturities and interest rates.

Series EE bond a U.S. government security issued at one-half par value, available in denominations of $50, $75, $100, $200, $500, $1,000, $5,000, and $10,000. The bond is non-transferrable and cannot be pledged as collateral. Minimum guaranteed interest is 7½ percent. Bonds held five years or more yield 85 percent of the average yield on other Treasury securities.

Series HH bond a U.S. government security that is purchased only by exchanging Series EE bonds with current market value of $500 or more. Maturity is 10 years, and interest is paid twice per year.

settlement date the date that ownership of securities is transferred.

sinking fund a reserve account established to accumulate funds to retire a future debt. A periodic payment to the fund, plus earnings, is calculated to produce the required maturity value of bond issues. The formula for a sinking fund is shown in Figure G–25.

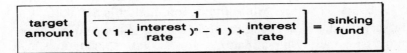

FIGURE G–25 Formula for Calculating Sinking Fund Periodic Deposits

split offering a single bond issue that contains both term and serial bonds.

spread the difference between the payment made by the investor for a bond and the amount the issuer receives, consisting of the concession and the takedown.

STRIPS Separate Trading of Registered Interest and Principal of Securities.

subordination the assignment of lower priority for one debt in comparison to another.

syndicate the organizations that will jointly underwrite a bond issue, representing the corporation and working through a selling group.

takedown the compensation paid to dealers by the syndicator for selling units of a new issue.

tax anticipation note (TAN) a mortgage note pledged by taxes to be received in the near future.

tax risk the risk that tax regulations or after-tax income will reduce the value of an investment, or that benefits available at the time an investment decision is made will change during the holding period.

10 percent guideline a general rule used by analysts stating that the total of bonded debt should be 10 percent or less of the market value of real estate in the area.

term bond a bond that contains a single maturity date and rate of interest, in contrast to a term bond, which has varying maturity dates and rates.

30-day visible supply a statistic published in the *Daily Bond Buyer* every Thursday reporting on municipal issues coming onto the market in the next 30 days.

TIGRs Treasury Investment Growth Receipts.

total yield the yield from a bond expanded to include an estimate of future income that includes compounding reinvested interest.

Treasury bill a short-term U.S. government debt with maturities of 13, 26, or 52 weeks. Minimum denomination is $10,000.

Treasury bond a U.S. government debt maturing beyond 10 years from issue date. Denominations are $1,000, $5,000, $10,000, $100,000, and $1 million.

Treasury note a U.S. government debt maturing between two and 10 years from issue date. Denominations are $1,000, $5,000, $10,000, $100,000, and $1 million.

20-bond index a statistic included in the *Daily Bond Buyer* summarizing average yields on highly rated bonds with 20-year maturities.

20 percent cushion rule a general rule used by analysts stating that the revenue from a facility should be higher than 20 percent of budgeted cash payments, including expenses, maintenance, and debt service. This creates a cushion for unexpected expenses.

25 percent rule a general rule used by analysts stating that a municipality's debt should not be greater than 25 percent of its total revenue budget.

underwriter the combination of companies that places a bond on the market, including the lead underwriter (investment banker) and the selling group.

unit investment trust (UIT) a trust that purchases a portfolio of bonds and sells units to investors. Bonds are not bought or sold, and investors receive periodic interest and, upon maturity, redemption value. The UIT is not managed actively.

unlimited tax bond a general obligation bond not restricted by the issuer's current taxing power. The issuer has the right to raise additional taxes, if necessary, to meet the bond obligation.

Western account a version of the syndicate agreement in which each member is responsible only for marketing a specified portion of a new issue. No one firm will be held responsible for marketing unsold units of other members in the syndicate.

Yellow Sheets a daily listing of markets in corporate debt securities, published by the National Quotation Bureau.

yield the percentage of return an investor receives, based on the amount invested or on the current market value of holdings.

yield curve the trend in a bond's total yield, which summarizes the effect of all buying and selling activity. Yield, price, and risk are taken into account. As a general rule, the yield curve rises during the short term and levels out when maturity date is farther away.

yield to maturity a calculation of yield that takes into consideration the discount of premium and the time until maturity.

zero coupon bond a bond issued at discount, with interest accreted during the period until maturity and with par value paid at maturity date.

Index